THE KING'S TROOP
Royal Horse Artillery

The King's Troop
ROYAL HORSE ARTILLERY

BY **MAJOR MCR WALLACE** RHA

Photographs by Kit Houghton
Drawings by Joan Wanklyn

THRESHOLD BOOKS

First published 1984 by Threshold Books Limited
661 Fulham Road, London SW6

ISBN 0 901366 41 2

Designed by John Mitchell
Printed in Great Britain
by Jolly & Barber Ltd, Rugby

This book has been produced
with the financial support
of Dewhurst, The Master Butcher

CONTENTS

BUCKINGHAM PALACE

This book tells the story of The King's Troop, Royal Horse Artillery from its origins to the present day.   That is a bald and wholly inadequate statement, although technically correct.   If you lived or were brought up in London, as I was, London ceremonial was part of your life and The King's Troop have been as much a part of my life as the Guards Division or Household Cavalry.   They have added immeasurably to the Summer in the city and all round the country; to the Royal Tournament and the Trooping of the Colour to the Essex County Show and recently as mounted stewards at the Gatcombe Park Horse Trials.   Firing Salutes or performing their spectacular musical drive, at home or abroad, they never fail to capture the imagination and command the respect of the public.

As with anything to do with animals there is always scope for the unexpected and occasions where the intelligence of certain members of the animal kingdom can be regarded as negligible or very advanced, rather depending on your relative involvement in that incident.

Major Wallace, as a raconteur of some note, has successfully transplanted the baldness of my original statement in filling it out with a comprehensive picture of the Troop's many activities from in front and behind the scenes, and dotted with human and equine characters.

The men who serve in The King's Troop are part of Britain's modern army and trained as such, but I think we can all be grateful to my Grandfather, King George VI, for his instigation of the Riding Troop in 1946 for the purpose of maintaining their ceremonial salute firing role, but after he visited them at "The Wood" he decreed that henceforward it should be known as "The King's Troop".   For all those people who have watched and wondered at The King's Troop performances, this book can only add to the respect and fondness with which they are regarded by so many.

Anne

List of Illustrations

PENINSULAR

WATERLOO

INDIA 1817

CHAPTER ONE

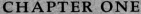

Origins

THE KING'S TROOP Royal Horse Artillery is the Saluting Battery of Her Majesty's Household Troops. It was formed in 1946 at the express wish of King George VI to fire Royal Salutes in Hyde Park on royal anniversaries and to take part in the other 'great ceremonies of state'.

Anyone watching the Troop gallop into action in Hyde Park, dismount at the canter, unhook and bring their guns into action in a matter of seconds, might be forgiven for thinking that these slick drills have been perfected purely for ceremonial reasons or to impress the tourists. Far from it. They are the legacy of drills 'fine tuned' over the years in the waging of war: the speed and precision being required of necessity, in order to inflict on the enemy maximum casualties for as long as possible. It is perhaps worthwhile to cast one's mind back nearly 200 years to the time when these drills were first evolved and their value became apparent.

As long ago as 1640, Gustavus Adolphus of Sweden introduced light, mobile guns in an effort to achieve rapid deployment of artillery. He in fact somewhat overdid this quest for mobility by constructing them of copper and leather with the result that on being fired they burst. British artillery, despite its undoubted excellence, was more static than its Continental counterparts, but by 1704 Marlborough was making use of artillery as a mobile weapon in his campaigns. According to the historian Fortescue,

> '... The Artillery came out of the war with no less, perhaps even more, brilliancy than the other corps of the army, and it is likely that no artillery officers ever worked more strenuously and skilfully in the face of enormous difficulties than the devoted men who brought their guns first down to the south side of the Danube and then back across the river to the battlefield of Blenheim ...'

Once the British Army appreciated the value of mobile artillery, experiments were tried, such as galloper guns (3-pounders) attached to infantry battalions but manned by gunners. The

The stables at Goodwood House were virtually the birthplace of the Royal Horse Artillery, as it was here that the third Duke of Richmond supervised the training of the first Troops, 'A' and 'B'. The magnificent stable quadrangle, designed for the Duke by William Chambers in the 1750s, has seen little change in 200 years. The photograph shows the private entrance to the stables from the house.

as they are today

only here until because of Queen & Monarchy.

use of galloper guns against the Hyder Ali of Mysore in the middle of the 18th century is well recorded, the guns belonging to the Madras Flying Artillery of the East India Company. In this instance, single guns drawn by driven horses (ie postillion-driven) with mounted detachments were attached to each regiment of cavalry and used as close support weapons in the style of Charles II of Sweden.

In 1759, however, after the battle of Minden, Frederick the Great had gone a stage further and formed what we know as troops of Horse Artillery. These were teams of horses driven by men on the near side with a limber and gun attached by means of traces. The detachment responsible for firing and servicing the piece was mounted on its own horses with an additional two 'limber gunners' riding on the limber itself. Frederick saw his Horse Artillery as a mobile reserve in the infantry's main battle, as well as supporting the fast-moving cavalry brigades.

Tribute was paid to the great professionalism of the British artillery at Minden, under the skilful handling of Captain Macbean, and it was probably the first time that we employed the concept of 'fire and manoeuvre' with success. '... The bold handling of his brigade by Captain Macbean, who followed up with his 'heavies' (ten 12-pounders), putting his horses to the

12

trot between successive positions and finally opening fire at short range on the retiring enemy, caused such disorder that forty-three guns and all the baggage were captured ... The rapidity of movement shown by the British gunners at Minden marked an important advance in artillery tactics.' (Graham.)

In 1716 the Duke of Marlborough was responsible for the formation of the first two regular Companies of Artillery. In 1722, the year in which he died, two more Companies were brought on to the establishment and the title 'The Royal Regiment of Artillery' was accorded. In 1756 the achievements of the Regiment were recognised by the granting of the privilege of taking the right of Foot and of dismounted Dragoons on all parades. Despite the fact that we were slightly behind some Continental neighbours in the light and mobile concept of artillery it is quite clear that the Gunners had earned a respected place in the British Army.

One of the main problems which reduced the efficiency of the Regiment in the 18th century was the use of hired civilian drivers used to move the guns. Although the companies of artillery were a well-organised and disciplined force – rightfully respected by Continental armies for their professional skills – they could not rely on the drivers and/or their horses. Neither civilians nor animals were necessarily trained for the rigours of warfare, and they behaved accordingly. The gunners themselves were dismounted, and trudged along behind the guns, moving only, at best, as fast as the infantry. It was not unknown for the officers, who were mounted, to bring the guns into action and then to await their detachments, who would arrive panting and breathless some time later.

I would not, however, wish to create the impression that the artillery of the 18th century was an unimaginative organisation. This was certainly not the case. Actions all over the world demonstrated their bravery, skill and professionalism, but it would appear that there was a requirement for faster moving and more mobile artillery to complement the guns which, though longer in range, were slow and heavy.

It was with this need in mind that the British Army debated the concept of horse artillery formations. In the 18th century, as in modern times, financial restrictions were a major stumbling block. As early as 1788 the idea had attracted the Master General of Ordnance, then responsible for the artillery arm, but it remained 'in committee' for a further five years before any decision was reached.

The man largely responsible for the creation of horse artillery in the British Army, which at this stage was the last of the leading European armies to adapt to it, was Charles, third Duke of Richmond and Lennox, who held the position of Master General of the Ordnance from 1782 to 1795.

Trumpeters c 1895. Boys were recruited at the age of 14 and after training at a depôt were posted to Batteries where they became the responsibility of the BSM. These two, probably the sons of men in the Regiment, are wearing the stable jacket which in basic pattern was the same for both officers and other ranks. The pill-box cap was worn, with minor variations, from 1864 to 1903.

1850

INDIA 1857

c.1861

1900

1923

1917

The Third Duke of Richmond, Master General of Ordnance and accepted 'Godfather' of Horse Artillery.

It was said by no less a person than the famous horse gunner General Mercer that the Duke was converted to the idea of highly mobile artillery after an incident which occurred in Southampton. Some French prisoners rioted on board a ship lying off-shore and there was no local artillery to assist in suppressing them. It is alleged that an enterprising gunner officer stationed at Winchester, harnessed a couple of 6-pounders to some post-horses, and galloped, with his detachments in post-chaises, to Southampton in time to quell the disturbance. Although there is considerable doubt as to the authenticity of this story, the important point is that the Master General became the accepted 'Godfather' of Horse Artillery and received two troops, A and B, in 1793. The Duke himself took a great personal interest in the raising of his Horse Artillery. He even had them at his own country seat at Goodwood in Sussex in order to watch over them and to influence their structure and training.

The new mounted branch of the Regiment was to be known as Royal Horse Artillery and was to be distinct from its parent, but at the same time integrated with it and controlled by its senior commanders. The officers (as now) did not join it permanently but rather were posted to their Troops for tours of duty and then returned to the Royal Artillery from whence they came. The rank and file could soldier longer than the officers, and, for continuity reasons, some remained permanently. The personnel, however, were selected for merit and efficiency – which right up to this present day has had a significant effect on the Royal Regiment as a whole and provides a talking point which can generate considerable heat!

The new Troops of Royal Horse Artillery were described as 'the most complete thing in the army'. They were a self-contained entity not dissimilar to the current King's Troop organisation. As they developed they varied considerably, but in general they were quite a large unit. Each troop contained 180 horses and men capable of moving and firing six guns. The guns were known as 'sub-divisions' (as opposed to 'subsections' in the King's Troop today) and were drawn by six horses in pairs, the near side ones being ridden by a driver. As in the rest of Europe, two gunners rode on the limber and eight others were individually mounted to form the detachment; each sub-division had its own ammunition wagon, similarly drawn. The divisions (two guns) were capable of independent action commanded by their subaltern officer (section commander), or as a troop split into three gun half-batteries, each of which was under command of a captain. In this way the much needed mobility and flexibility were achieved.

In addition to the 'teeth' of the troop, already described, a comprehensive back-up was provided. Each unit had its own

Staff-Sergeant Christopher Carnagan (SM) was the BSM of 'D' Battery RHA at St John's Wood in 1895. It is interesting to note some of the changes that have been made since his time: his horse (probably about 16 hands) has a mane and banged tail at the bottom of the dock; it is wearing a charger-style headcollar, breastplate, and sheepskin saddle-cover; a white rope has now replaced the chain. Carnagan is wearing a slightly curved cavalry-type sword, and his lines are on the left-hand side (changed to the right in 1951 at the request of King George VI).

The Battery, which sailed for Bombay on 26 October 1898 was in those days equipped with six 12pdr breech-loading guns.

organic baggage train, a wheel-wagon complete with a wheelwright, plus farriers, harness-makers, artificers and even a surgeon. This 'complete' unit allowed a large degree of independence from the troops which it was supporting, and so in turn permitted it to change its support as and when ordered so to do: a far cry from the 'crawling peasant-driven teams of the late 18th century Field Batteries'. (Duncan.)

Because of the emphasis on mobility for which Troops of Royal Horse Artillery were raised, it is often said that they were organised solely to support cavalry. Although not specifically intended for this purpose, it was without doubt a job which the new troops did extremely well. Not only could they keep their guns (6-pounders) within range during the fast-moving cavalry battle; they could also delay coming out of action until the last possible minute, before galloping away and coming into action again elsewhere. The effect of the deadly case-shot at short range was devastating, and the ability to allow the enemy to close to only a few hundred yards before annihilating them, often proved to be decisive – as demonstrated by Bull's Troop at Fuentes d'Onoro in the Peninsular Campaign.

However, the new horse artillery Troops were not designed to be fast versions of the existing field batteries; they were a totally new concept based on their ability to move rapidly. As a result of actions by the Royal Horse Artillery, the rest of the artillery arm was re-structured to do likewise, though to a somewhat limited degree. In 1801, only eight years after A Troop's formation by the Duke of Richmond, the Corps of Gunner Drivers was created; in 1806 it became the Corps of Artillery Drivers. The first step towards modelling the rest of the artillery on the RHA was a very important one. It meant that civilian drivers and requisitioned animals could be dispensed with, and that the artillery corps could train their own men and horses and could allocate them to parts of artillery as required. It was in 1822 that drivers finally became an integral part of all units. Historians stress that neither the men nor the horses of the field artillery could match the excellence of the new horse artillery formations.

It is not surprising that these men and horses were of such high quality. Both had a very difficult job to do. The detachment which served the guns had a variety of drills to perform in order to bring the piece into action, before firing rapidly and accurately. A large number of complicated and sometimes dangerous items of equipment had to be prepared and maintained for the successful firing of each round. Similar drills had to be carried out by the field artillery companies, but as a general rule the RHA had to be considerably quicker. As well as carrying out these complicated manoeuvres the men also trained in cavalry drills, which they often used. All members of a sub-division were expected to be as proficient with a sabre as the cavalry which they supported. At the Battle of Jaora Alipore, Leslie's Troop of the Bombay Horse Artillery under the command of Captain Lightfoot, having engaged the enemy at a range of 250 yards, mounted their detachments and charged alongside (and even in front of) the cavalry.

The drivers, too, unarmed initially, were skilled men. In order to fit their light draught horses they were usually the smallest personnel in the troop, and they had to ride as well – if not better – than any horseman in the army. So that they could acquire the expertise necessary to manoeuvre themselves, the teams trained hard together: six horses, three men and limber gunners 'tied' together, with a ton and a half of bucking gun and limber, across rough country at the gallop while possibly under fire.

The horses, it is recorded, had to be 'four to six years old when bought, short-legged, open-chested and broad-winded; not to exceed 15 hands 2 inches, nor, if under four years old, to be less than 15 hands $\frac{1}{2}$-inch; to have good bone and action'. The description fits well the average type of horse in the King's Troop today. Unfortunately prices now are higher than in earlier times, when, at 30 guineas a horse, it cost about £5,000 to mount a troop of horse artillery. Then, as now, all these horses had to be located, vetted, tested for suitability, and bought. After this they were to be backed and broken to 'ordinary' standards before breaking for draught harness.

Despite the fact that the Royal Artillery wisely selected its best officers to serve with the RHA, it was never intended to raise a corps d'élite, although at the time that was very much in vogue with the infantry. However, a large number of the officers selected were well trained, highly motivated men, who rose to the top of their profession, such as Generals Mercer, Ross, Gardiner and Downmans. They, along with the 'God-father' of the RHA, the benevolent Master General of the Ordnance, were responsible for setting a standard of excellence recognised by other arms – a standard maintained to this day by their successors.

As the new Troops displayed their prowess and proved their worth, so the horse artillery concept was developed, and more Troops were raised as the years went by. Altogether 14 such 'complete' Troops were 'carefully and lovingly created' between 1793 and 1811.

Meanwhile in India the East India Company developed its own Horse Artillery battery. It had been authorised to raise companies of Field Artillery in 1748 and was not slow to emulate the British Horse Artillery, the first being formed as the 1st Bengal Troop in 1800 as part of the Experimental Brigade, which went to Egypt the following year.

The three provinces of Bengal, Bombay and Madras all raised troops of Horse Artillery, beautifully mounted and immaculately turned out in their distinctive uniforms. They employed their guns in a most dashing way by galloping ahead of the line of battle and coming into action at point blank range to subdue the enemy's defence before the infantry's assault. In all, 17 'European' and six 'Native' Troops were raised.

The newly raised troops of RHA in the British Army were in action in a number of contrasting theatres soon after their formation. They fought in such places as Ireland, Holland, Buenos Aires and the Peninsular Campaigns. They were thus ready to prove their expertise in the final campaign of the Napoleonic Wars.

It seems fitting at this point to include a brief account of one of the most famous horse artillery actions, namely that of Mercer's G Troop at the Battle of Waterloo. Although this celebrated and well documented action is one of the best known episodes of the famous conflict, it would be wrong to think that Mercer won the artillery battle on his own. Thirteen troops and brigades of artillery were engaged – eight troops of RHA (six of which were initially uncommitted) and five field companies.

The artillery troops and brigades were positioned on a ridge behind the infantry at 100-yard intervals – with the exception of Whinyates Rocket Troop RHA, which was some 500 yards to the east of the artillery line – so that they covered a distance of about 1200 yards. They had one single aim – which was to inflict maximum casualties on the attacking cavalry and infantry as they advanced up the slope to assault the Allies. The Duke's 'categoric instructions' were that they should withdraw into the infantry squares as and when the enemy broke through to them, and then return to their guns after a successful counter-attack. The enemy would certainly break through, as their numbers were greater and their morale was high. The gunners were ordered not to waste their valuable ammunition on counter-battery fire.

Thus the scene was set for one of the most decisive battles in the history of the British Army. We shall now turn to Captain Mercer (as he then was) and follow his account of the action.

Mercer's Troop was deployed on the extreme right and was summoned (with Ramsay's Troop) to counter the threat of a French cavalry charge in the centre. Mercer was led by Sir Augustus Frazer to the position which his guns were to occupy with an opening cry of 'left limber up and as fast as you can'. Shortly afterwards his Troop assembled and Mercer was able to cry in turn 'at the gallop, march!'. Mercer himself takes up the story:

'I rode with Frazer, whose face was as black as a chimney sweep's from the smoke, the jacket sleeve of his right arm torn open by a musket ball or case-shot, which had merely grazed the flesh. As we went along he told me that the French had assembled an enormous mass of cavalry ... and that in all probability we should immediately be charged on gaining our position.' The Duke's orders, however, were positive: "In the event of their persevering and charging home, you do not expose your men but retire with them into the adjacent squares of infantry" (an order unlikely to appeal to Mercer who had already engaged in counter-battery fire, thus breaking the Duke's other "categoric instructions"). 'As he spoke we were ascending the reverse slope of the main position and we breathed a new atmosphere – the air was suffocatingly hot, resembling that issuing from an oven. We were enveloped in thick smoke, and *malgré* the incessant roar of cannon and musketing, could distinctly hear round us a mysterious humming noise, like that which one hears of a summer's evening proceeding from myriads of black-beetles; common-shot, too, ploughed the ground in all directions, and so thick were the trails of balls and bullets that it seemed dangerous to extend the arm lest it should be torn off' ... 'Our first gun had scarcely gained the interval of their (the Brunswickers) squares, when I saw through the smoke the leading squadrons of the enemy coming at a brisk trot ... I immediately ordered the line to be formed for action – "Case-shot!" – and the leading gun was unlimbered and commenced firing almost as soon as the word was given ...'

The French cavalry were at this stage some 100 yards away, advancing at the trot. The first gun reduced them to a walk, and subsequent rounds of the vicious shot reduced them to mounds of dead horses and men. Mercer felt that he could not contemplate obeying Wellington's orders. He was obviously causing heavy casualties, and should he leave his guns to withdraw to the infantry square, the French cavalry would sabre his men between the guns and the Brunswick infantry. According to Mercer the Brunswickers looked very unsteady and might panic in this their first battle if they saw him leave his guns. The guns fired and fired again until the French were fighting their way to the rear. Wave after wave of brave French cavalrymen and horses were met by this onslaught of fire which Mercer's Horse Gunners kept producing in a rhythmic drill. Gradually a rampart of dead men and horses grew in front of his gun muzzles and here he stayed until the last charge of the Imperial Guard was broken and the ominous cry of 'La Garde récule' signalled the final collapse of their repeated assaults on the Allied line.

It is estimated that the combined guns of the horse and field artillery fired a total of 10,000 rounds during the battle – an average of 129 rounds per gun. From these figures it is reasonable to expect that they inflicted some 10,000 of the 30,000 casualties suffered by the French. During the attack by d'Erlons' corps alone, when all but two of the British batteries fired continuously at the advancing mass of infantry, it is estimated that the guns killed 3,000 men. It is not surprising that Napoleon himself, after the battle, said ... 'C'est avec l'artillerie qu'on fait la guerre'.

The battle, however, was not without loss on the British side. Four of the Artillery Commanders – Bean, Bolton, Ramsay and Lloyd – were killed or died of their wounds; 265 all ranks (and 309 horses) were killed or wounded – a casualty rate of 13 per cent of those in battle. British guns therefore can be said to have acquitted themselves worthily at Waterloo and in just 23 years the formation of Horse Artillery had proved to be a success and a significant milestone in the history of the Royal Regiment.

After Wellington's success at Waterloo there followed a period of peace, virtually unbroken until the beginning of the Crimean War in 1854. Horse Artillery participation in the Crimea was comparatively small, considering the large numbers of cavalry involved. Probably the most notable action by the RHA was C Battery's involvement during the charge of the Heavy Brigade at Balaclava on 25 October 1854.

On returning from an all-night picquet, C Battery, under command of Major John Brandling, was ordered to join the Heavy Brigade in their charge of the Russian cavalry. C Battery came into action on the right rear of the British cavalry. Fortunately for the British, the Russians had left their horse artillery out of battle, and during the *melée* after the British charge, only hand-to-hand and sabre fighting took place. It was not until the British cavalry had given up chasing the Russians – who quickly reorganised themselves after the close combat – that Brandling used his deadly guns. At a range of half a mile he fired 49 rounds of shot and case into the Russian cavalry. The effect was devastating. The action lasted only a matter of minutes, but had a profound effect on the results of the battle. The Russians fled, shocked and broken, with C Battery giving chase and firing again until they in turn were engaged by a Russian battery. C limbered up once more and tried to support the ill-fated charge of the Light Brigade. However, without clear orders, and practically immobilised by worn-out horses, Brandling could do little to influence the outcome.

The last action by C on this longest of days (they'd been without food or rest for 36 hours) was to dispel some pursuing Russian cavalry. Once again the RHA had contributed to the outcome in a manner totally disproportionate to its numbers.

Only four years after Balaclava, Horse Artillery batterys also played a distinguished part in the final operations to quell the Indian Mutiny. One of the most famous actions was the cavalry charge of E Troop (now D Battery) at Secundra Gunge, where they routed a large number of mutineers – sabering over 200 of them. As far as the Royal Horse Artillery was concerned the principal effect of the mutiny was that the European Horse Artillery of the old East India Company was successfully absorbed into the RHA in 1861.

In briefly tracing the history of the RHA from its inception to the present day the next major campaign worthy of mention is the Second Afghan War, which took place some 20 years after the Queen's Proclamation in India. There is no space here to describe the events leading up to, nor to give the details of, the continued mismanagement of this arduous campaign, but mention must be made of the Battle of Maiwand in 1880 which, as well as collective gallantry on the part of E/B Battery, produced two notable VCs.

The Battery found itself supporting a small force of three battalions – one British and two Indian – and two Indian cavalry regiments. The opposition consisted of 20,000 Afghan regulars, plus a horde of fanatical tribesmen. Despite a some-what unsuitable battle formation, the British force was holding out well – until one of the battalions broke and ran. Immediately, the Afghans took advantage of the disorder, broke through the infantry ranks, and closed on the 9-pounders of E/B, who were firing case at point-blank range. As the guns were almost overrun, Slade, the Battery Captain, sent for what was left of the gun teams (67 horses had already been killed by the Afghan counter-battery fire) and ordered 'Mount'. Surrounded by screaming tribesmen, the guns, in retreat, withdrew and came into action again at 400-yard intervals until they finally disengaged themselves. There followed a long and thirsty trek back to Kandahar under the most trying conditions. The Battery received no fewer than two Victoria Crosses and nine Distinguished Conduct Medals.

The last campaign of the 19th century in which the RHA took part was the South African War. The British Army, sticking to the drills and formations of past campaigns, was pitted against the fieldcraft of the hard riding and accurate rifle fire of the Boers. British guns, including two new ones, the 12- and larger 15-pounders, could only fire shrapnel, designed for the massed targets of European conflicts rather than the well dug-in pockets of Boers.

Two actions which stand out as examples of extreme gallantry are those at Colenso and Sanna's Post. Both were concerned with the endeavour of 'saving the guns', which throughout the

'Saving the Guns' at the Battle of Maiwand, Second Afghan War.

The NCOs of 'O' Battery, The Rocket Troop, Bangalore, 1908. The Battery spent ten years in India before returning to England in 1912. They were in France throughout the Great War, returning to Aldershot in 1919. They served at The Wood from September 1923 until October 1926 where they were commanded by Major (Bt-Lt-Col) A K Main, DSO, who wrote the notes on 'Jones' which appear at the end of this book.

history of the Regiment has inspired the greatest courage. The Colenso action is included here because of its unique link with The King's Troop. In this incident, directly concerned with the relief of Ladysmith, Corporal Nurse of the 66th Battery RFA, among others, helped to save two guns when in full view of the withering fire of the Boers situated on the high ground beyond the Tugela River. As a result of his extreme bravery in the face of heavy enemy fire, Nurse and two officers were awarded the Victoria Cross. It is interesting to note that this contentious incident, although considered a disaster at the time, forced the enemy into action and thus prevented them from springing an ambush which would have been disastrous to the entire British force. Corporal Nurse's great, great grandson, Gunner Andrew Charles Colenso Nurse, is currently serving in the Troop as a trumpeter.

Sanna's Post, which took place in the year 1900, involved Q Battery RHA, and was also brought about through a cunning ambush by the Boers. U Battery was caught in a Boer trap and captured, virtually to a man. Q, from an exposed gun position, came into action in an effort to save the day. Again, the accurate sniper fire of the enemy, at nearly 1000 yards' range, caused heavy casualties among the gunners and their horses. Bravery of the highest order was displayed in an effort to withdraw the guns to more concealed positions. After several hours of fighting only one sergeant, one corporal and eight gunners remained unwounded. They attempted to manhandle the guns to safety; four made it. It was decided to treat this action as a case of collective gallantry, and one officer, one NCO and two gunners were individually awarded the VC.

The best documented action by an RHA Battery during the Great War took place at Néry in France on 1 September 1914. L Battery, in support of the 1st Cavalry Brigade, were hooked in but with draught poles on the ground, when the dense overnight fog lifted and 12 German guns in support of the 4th Cavalry Division opened fire on them at close range. It is difficult to describe the carnage among men and horses that followed this surprise attack; the dead and dying lay everywhere as the Battery attempted to reorganise itself. Three guns were brought into action by the Battery Captain, his subalterns, and some gunners. Immediately two guns were knocked out and most of the depleted crews killed. One gun managed to continue firing for an hour, until eventually even it was silenced; it did, however, buy time for reinforcements, supported by I Battery RHA, to come on the scene and put the Germans to flight. For their selfless sacrifice three members of L Battery received the VC.

It was appropriate that on 24 March 1918 the last successful horsed charge against a modern enemy should have been supported by an RHA Battery. O, in support of General Harman's cavalry force, covered the rally and withdrawal of a skilfully executed flank attack in which the enemy was routed with great loss.

The Great War signalled the end of horse-drawn artillery: a new kind of warfare, in which, mercifully, horses have no place, was slowly developing. However, a considerable number of years were to pass before they were phased out altogether, and until engines and tanks finally took their place, they suffered most horribly.

As the rest of the Army mechanised between the World Wars so did the RHA, though not without a certain amount of passive resistance. It is said that while 'progress' was being made elsewhere, the Horse Gunners continued to play polo and hunt in preference to adapting their skills to modern warfare. However, in the '30s, when the writing was plainly on the wall and the cavalry mechanised, the RHA followed suit, with the usual efficiency and enthusiasm. The last Battery to mechanise was K, carrying out ceremonial duties at St John's Wood until 1939.

During World War II the RHA took on a variety of roles and equipments. The Royal Regiment of Artillery grew enormously in size until it was even larger than the Royal Navy. As a result, Horse Artillery batteries were raised and played their part in a great many actions in contrasting conditions and theatres of war. There were, for example, no fewer than 30 Royal Horse Artillery batteries in North Africa alone, and it was here that the RHA received their only VC awarded while serving the guns. Early on in the campaign the Horse Gunners took on the anti-tank role, with both 2- and 25-pounders. It was not an enviable task. Neither of these guns was a match for a tank, and such inequality resulted in outstanding feats of heroism – but also, sadly, in great loss of life.

At Sidi Rezegh in the Western Desert, J Battery was in support of the Rifle Brigade when it was attacked by at least 60 tanks. Second-Lieutenant Ward Gunn was observed walking about his gun position directing the fire of his three 2-pounders and one Bofors, all of which were coming under a murderous fire from the approaching enemy. Eventually only one of these tiny anti-tank guns was operable; it was on a burning vehicle which had no armour. Gunn, aided by Major Pinney of M Battery, continued to fire at the enemy until he was hit in the forehead and killed instantly. He received a posthumous VC.

After the War, when the Army was greatly reduced in numbers, there was considerable discussion within the Royal Regiment as to whether the RHA system was still required. Did the regiment need a corps d'élite, and if so, what role should it adopt? Fortunately, common sense prevailed, and a number of RHA regiments were retained. Some have since lost their RHA status as the Royal Regiment has been reduced, in order to keep them as a small proportion of the regiment as a whole. There are currently three RHA regiments in service – two in Germany and one in the United Kingdom. Additionally, the King's Troop RHA remains at The Wood, and serves to remind the batteries of the Regiment, whatever their discipline or their origins that at one time they, like the Troop, were all horsed.

CHAPTER TWO

Formation

IT IS NO COINCIDENCE that very soon after the formation of the first Royal Horse Artillery Troops it was decided to raise an organisation that should be responsible for equestrian standards within the Royal Regiment. The formation of the Riding Establishment was announced in the following letter from the Deputy Adjutant General:

> Sir. – Captain C A Quist will be appointed Riding Master to the Ordnance Department of horses and commence the duties of this office on 1 January 1803. The three subalterns, now mustered in his company, are to be attached to him, to assist in carrying on the duties he is intended to preside over. In order to commence the formation of a Riding House Establishment, the Master General directs that 20 men may be selected from the Gunners and Drivers, and mustered in Captain Quist's Company in addition to those now in it. Captain Quist is to have besides, authority to enlist others, or to exchange any who may appear upon trial to be unpromising. In respect to horses, the Master General would consider for the present about 12 necessary to be obtained. As fast as Captain Quist procures them, they are to be mustered as employed in the Riding House and foraged on the Establishment of Gunner Drivers.
>
> I have (etc)
> (Signed) J MACLEOD
> *20 December 1802*

So Captain Quist, an elderly German from Hanover, was 'imported' to be the first Riding Master of the Royal Artillery on the express orders of King George III. It has been said that the horsemanship for which the Royal Horse Artillery became renowned was largely influenced by the cavalry of the King's German Legion. Quist, who was not commissioned until he was 71 years of age, was a student of the famous Spanish Riding School at Vienna and brought with him many of the Continental methods of training horses and riders. He was well known for working horses between the pillars, as practised in Vienna, and the Troop's own cypher includes a horse between two

Captain C A Quist, first Superintendent and Riding Master to the Riding House Establishment, 1803. This painting, which hangs in the Officers' Mess at St John's Wood, depicts Quist with his remarkable horse Wonder, who lived until he was 40. His gravestone, along with those of other famous chargers, stands only 30 yards away from the Mess, by the manège.

pillars as a testimony to Quist's equestrian skills.

The Riding Establishment was formed at Woolwich on 20 September 1803, and for five years was borne on the strength of the Corps of Royal Artillery Drivers. In 1808 the Troop was established as an independent unit and until 1856 was part of the Horse Brigade. It continued as Royal Horse Artillery when the rest of the Regiment left the jurisdiction of the Master General of the Ordnance and came under the control of the War Office in 1857. Twenty years later the Troop was brought into the establishment of the Royal Artillery once again, but quickly reverted to Royal Horse Artillery in 1903.

Captain Quist continued as the first Superintendent and Commander of the Troop until he died on 26 December 1821 at the age of 91 years; his horse 'Wonder' lived to see his 41st year, and his gravestone is now to be seen at The Wood, along with those of other distinguished chargers.

The first Riding Master was posted to the Troop in 1858, and in 1873 the Captain Superintendent was replaced by a Major Superintendent. It is interesting to note that this rather splendid old-fashioned rank lasted until 1947. When Lieutenant-Colonel H K Gillson RHA formed the Riding Troop in 1946 he was known as the Superintendent. It was only when the King visited the following year that he decreed that the Major in command should be known as the Officer Commanding.

In its early days the Troop was established to improve the quality of horsemanship within the Regiment and for the training of officers' chargers. We see from the Records of the Royal Artillery Military Academy the following entry dated 5 April 1830: 'A Riding Squad composed of the ten senior Corporals or Cadets off duty to attend the Riding School on Mondays and Fridays at half past twelve o'clock. The first introduction of riding as part of the instruction at the Royal Military Academy.' The Troop therefore was responsible for teaching the Gentlemen Cadets at the 'Shop', as the Academy was known. Horses used by the Cadets for the various Inter-Company and Inter-Academy/College competitions were also provided by the Troop.

When the Troop had its establishment increased it was entrusted with the training of officers and NCOs in all branches of equitation, instead of leaving the greater part of this work to the specialist Riding Master or NCO Rough Riders. This situation continued until the Troop was split into two parts and much of its work transferred to Weedon to be finally absorbed into the Army School of Equitation in 1922. It was then that the Troop lost its 'Riding Masters', which had been a rank in the RHA and RA; it was something similar to a Quartermaster's commission in that all Riding Masters were commissioned from the ranks. The only Riding Master's appointment which has survived to this day is that of the Household Cavalry Mounted Regiment.

The Riding Troop was at its busiest during the Great War. In 1915, the Troop, or at least elements of it, moved into St John's Wood Barracks, north-west London, as part of B Reserve Brigade RHA. They had to requisition a fair-sized proportion of the sacred turf at Lord's Cricket Ground (half a mile away) to accommodate the horses needed for the teaching of so many officers and NCOs to ride. It is hard to imagine when watching a modern-day Test Match that the beautifully manicured ground once housed loose jumping lanes and was being used from dawn till dusk seven days a week!

The Troop adapted itself to the requirements of the day. In addition to training the Gentlemen Cadets at the 'Shop', the Boys of the Depôt Brigade, and the young officers from the Royal Naval College at Greenwich, they also supplied a great number of horses for a variety of occasions such as the Army Council, Dominion representatives and Foreign Attachés at the Ceremony of Trooping the Colour on His Majesty's Birthday. On 16 July 1919 all RHA detachments were mounted by the Troop and as many as 38 horses were supplied as officers' chargers. When His Majesty King George V visited Woolwich, the home of the Regiment (and of the Riding Troop for over 100 years) on 9 April 1918, the Troop supplied the Sovereign's Escort.

Duties of a different nature had to be carried out in 1921

An RHA Gun Team *c* 1904. This photograph, probably taken in Ireland, shows a team equipped with a 12-pdr 6cwt breech-loading gun. The horses still have manes (other than chargers, only remounts at The Wood retain their manes) but the harness is the same as that used by the Troop today.

during the Coal Strike and in 1926 when the General Strike took place. Guards and picquets over persons and property were carried out by the Troop at both Weedon and Woolwich.

Personnel within the Riding Troop also took part, with some considerable success, in show-jumping competitions, horse trials, point-to-points and National Hunt racing. All these equestrian skills, including of course participation in the hunting field, were very actively taught and encouraged at Weedon where the Riding Establishment Royal Horse Artillery found itself early in 1919. It is said that the legendary Weedon, about which all horsemen enviously hear from the 'old and bold', was the brainchild of Major CT (Taffy) Walwyn, DSO. In the words of Major-General EB (Dolly) de Fonblanque, himself a great Horse Gunner, he is reputed to have 'penetrated into the War Office as far as a major could hope to do and delivered himself of words to the following effect:

"The standard of riding in the Royal Regiment is deplorable; the erstwhile cavalry barracks at Weedon are now empty; I suggest that a riding establishment be set up with the object of training young officers and NCOs to teach riding in their units in place of the Riding Masters and Rough Riders of yore. I further suggest that I be Chief Instructor of such establishment."

Almost miraculously it was so!'
The Riding Establishment therefore moved into a new and

29

This photograph, taken c 1903, possibly on Okehampton ranges, shows an RHA detachment laying a twelve-pounder. One of the new generation of breech-loading guns developed in the 1890s and used in the Boer War, it could fire a 12½lb shrapnel shell 5600 yards.

here

tracing @ weedon

famous era. Walwyn selected four Horse Gunner officers and a few Warrant officers and senior NCOs to form his opening team of instructors; Lieutenant-Colonel (Jack) Livingstone-Learmonth was in command. He also brought up three of the Woolwich Riding Masters from the other half of the Troop and put them through a three-month course to 'imprint on them his methods and technique' and to gain from them what they might have to give in regard to Riding School drills. They then returned to Woolwich. Concurrently, during the early months of 1919 two main undertakings were simultaneously taking place. They built up a large stock of horses, mostly from Ireland, and worked hard to develop the 250-odd acres of land available into an outdoor training area with an abundance of manèges, arenas, and cross-country obstacles. The hilly pasture-land lent itself to such an undertaking. It was intersected with timbered fences and hedges, had a stream running throughout its length and a curious 'fault' with near vertical sides; a veritable cross-country paradise!

The first course started in 1919 and the syllabus was remarkably similar to the Long Military Equitation Course which is still in existence. The allocation system was originally, and still is, designed to give a student a thorough knowledge of all aspects of riding. The students were issued with an unbroken 'remount', a half-trained (last season's remount) and a fully-trained animal. Each student rode his trained horse twice a day and his half-trained and remount once. During the week this riding was interspersed with lectures, demonstrations, visits, farriery, veterinary work, and fencing in the gymnasium. Apart from the latter, the initial course at Weedon in 1919 sounds similar in every way to those at Melton Mowbray some 60 years later.

One feature of the course was undoubtedly the emphasis

Firing a twelve-pounder. The breech-loader incorporated a 'spade', which absorbed recoil and which can be seen dug into the ground below the breech. This gun was followed by the thirteen-pounder QF piece, the main RHA armament during the Great War and now in service (for ceremonial purposes only) with the King's Troop.

The 13-pdr QF piece was the main RHA armament during the Great War and now in service (for ceremonial purposes only) with the King's Troop.

RHA Limbering Up. The drivers and detachments are in khaki service dress. Introduced in 1902, this was made of loose-fitting drab mixture serge. The peakless 'Broderick' cap, which appeared a year later, lasted only for two years, departing, unmourned, in 1905 to be replaced by a peaked cap similar to that worn by officers, which remains in service today with the mounted units.

placed on hunting. Weedon, like Melton, was in the centre of excellent hunting country surrounded by famous sporting packs such as the Pytcheley, Grafton and Warwickshire. Officers hunted two days a week to develop 'an eye for the country and test their reactions in difficult circumstances.' It also developed a keen sense of self preservation! Sadly, for a number of reasons hunting no longer flourishes at the Army School of Equitation as it used to in days gone by, despite its location as the 'capital' of fox hunting. The chase undoubtedly gives a rider a more secure seat in the saddle and a better understanding of a horse's ability – particularly useful for an officer on mounted duty with the King's Troop, and more so if his previous riding experience is slight.

In 1923, after much discussion, the Cavalry School at Netheravon and the Riding Establishment RHA merged to form the Army School of Equitation. Thus half the old Riding Troop ceased to exist in its original format but the other half at

Woolwich flourished until the outbreak of World War II in 1939, when it was disbanded by Major N H Kindersley.

After the War it was decided that the practice of firing Royal Salutes on State occasions should be continued. It was in fact the express wish of King George VI that it should be so. A letter from his Principal Private Secretary arrived at Headquarters Director Royal Artillery with the following message:

> 'The King would like the practice to be resumed on his next birthday; and His Majesty hopes that by then the saluting battery, usually stationed in St John's Wood, will have reverted to its pre-war status as a Royal Horse Artillery Battery with the appropriate uniform.'

His Majesty was referring to the succession of RHA Batteries which since 1880 had been stationed at St John's Wood Barracks (or 'The Wood' as it is affectionately known) to carry out the duties of Saluting Battery in London, as well as performing the Musical Drive at the Royal Tournament and other great military shows. Batteries used to carry out this three-year tour of ceremonial duty before returning to their normal duties with a Brigade or Regiment; the last to carry out this pleasant task was K Battery RHA, mechanised from The Wood as late as September 1939.

After six years of total immersion in warfare it was a lot to expect that the skills and splendour of those previous decades could be reproduced in a matter of months. 'Know-how' and the appropriate artillery were thin on the ground, while horses

'A' Battery, The Chestnut Troop, with their 'Light Dragon' tracked gun tower, Number 26 trailer, and 4.5'' howitzer on a MK 1 PA carriage. This was taken in 1938 at Aldershot, after their return the previous year from Egypt, where they had been mechanized in 1935.

'K' Battery, 1939. This is one of the last-ever photographs taken of a horsed battery. It shows 'K' Battery in the late summer of 1939 at St John's Wood, with the old Victorian barrack blocks in the background. 'K', who had been at The Wood since '36 had their last mounted parade in Regent's Park on 4 September 1939 and then moved in November to Wootton-under-Edge in Gloucestershire, where they formed 5 RHA as 'G' and 'K' Batteries. The horses were returned to the Army Horse-Collecting Centre, Melton Mowbray.

were also a rarity. However, the task ahead was a welcome one and by May 1946, plans to raise 'The Riding Troop' were well under way; Lieutenant-Colonel HK Gillson was nominated Superintendent. And so the tenuous link between the old Riding House Establishment of 1803 and the present-day Troop was maintained.

Officers, NCOs and men with pre-war experience were found and posted to join the Troop at its temporary base in Shoeburyness where the only 'active' stables remained. The horses there were used in draught to go out on to the mud flats to collect the spent shells from the Experimental Establishment. These were joined by a number of elderly horses found in various Remount Depôts, and between them formed the 'horse-power' for the new Troop. The staff at Shoeburyness were a great help to the foundation of the Troop and some of their men and horses actually took part in the first Birthday Salute.

In May 1946 the Troop moved to St John's Wood where 59 horses and 110 men squeezed into the old barracks. Work continued in earnest to prepare for the first salute only weeks away. Manèges became manèges again; the riding school lost its gymnasium-like appearance, and once again had 'hairies'

This photograph of the Riding Troop formed up at St John's Wood Barracks for the first post-War Salute, on 13 June 1946, clearly shows the old lines on the edge of the square, with the Riding School in the background and the Officers' Mess and lawn (now gone) in the top right-hand corner. The guns were 18-pounders, as enough 13-pounders could not be found. Two men from each detachment rode on the limbers because of a shortage of horses, but the Leaders, Centres and Wheelers, a splendid type of light Irish draught – the classic mould for an RHA horse – are beautifully matched. Note that the officers' chargers have neither sheepskins nor shabraques with their saddles.

trotting round it; harness was assembled, and guns were made serviceable. At this stage only 18-pounder guns could be used as the Troop was not equipped with the traditional 13-pounders, which it still has, until the following year.

After a considerable amount of hard work, self-help and determination, on 13 June 1946, six gun teams, served by a mixture of old pre-war Horse Gunners, and young, totally inexperienced drivers and detachments fired a 41-gun salute in honour of His Majesty's Birthday. They went in and out of action at the walk; gunners were mounted on the limbers; and the guns were not of the correct calibre; but the object had been achieved, and a magnificent job had been done by all ranks.

Progress was rapid. During the summer of that first year more horses were obtained, and expertise developed. More salutes were fired, this time at the canter, and work progressed

His Majesty King George VI with officers of the Troop during his visit on 24 October 1947.

towards performing the famous Musical Drives of yesteryear by the following summer. After a winter of serious training the first Drive took place at Aldershot in the summer of 1947 and the General Officer Commanding London District held his administrative inspection. Already the programme of those early days looks very much the same as the one on the wall behind me as I write.

Later that year, on 24 October, King George VI visited the Troop, and an historic event took place out of which the The King's Troop Royal Horse Artillery was born. Although the old Riding Troop had been inspected on three occasions this century by a reigning monarch (1908, 1916 and 1928) it was the first time that the old barracks at The Wood had been privileged to host such a visit. The inspection, with the Troop in full dress on the square, went extremely well. The King asked during a pre-lunch drink if the Troop would like to be called 'The King's Battery'? The Superintendent at this time, Major J A Norman, asked daringly if it could be 'The King's Troop' to which His Majesty agreed with the words 'All right, so long as it's mine I don't mind what you call it!'. Later, when signing the visitors' book, he crossed out 'Riding' and inserted 'King's'. The King's Troop therefore was officially designated, and it is the will of Her Majesty Queen Elizabeth II that the title should be retained during her reign, as a tribute to her father, to whom the Troop owes so much.

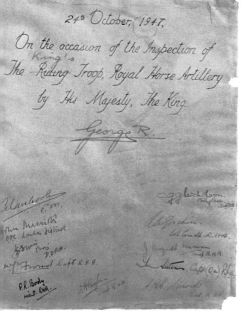

One of The Wood's most prized possessions: the document, written by Major (then Lieutenant) Eddie Boylan, which recorded the visit of King George VI in October 1947 and on which The King made his alteration to the Troop's name.

35

CHAPTER THREE

The Wood

No story about the King's Troop could be complete without outlining the history of its home, St John's Wood Barracks. 'The Wood' and the Troop are synonymous, and anyone fortunate enough to have served there will always remember the barracks with great affection. Many people are still unaware that the barracks even exist, hidden in the heart of one of London's most pleasant residential areas.

The origins of the barracks date back to 1804, when a Brigade of Artillery was stationed near the Master Gunner's House in St James' Park. A farm at St John's Wood was taken over by the Board of Ordnance as a billet for a detachment of the Corps of Gunner Drivers and their horses. It is hard to imagine that in those days the metropolis of London itself stretched only as far north as the site of the Marylebone Road. From that northern boundary the land was largely given over to dairy farming, and the site of the present barracks was one such farm, owned by the Eyre family who are still the ground landlords, in the name of the Eyre Estates. At the time of the Ordnance Board's request for accommodation, however, the signs of change were already evident. The days of cows and meadows were obviously numbered in an area so close to the capital, and the shrewd Eyres let part of the farm for the needs of the Regiment. Thus began the story of The Wood over 150 years ago at a rent of £150 per annum.

Details of life for those first few years at the 'Gunner Drivers Barracks' are not well documented. It is clear, however, that military duties were not strictly adhered to, despite a requirement for instant response in the event of a war, or 'domestic problems', and that the horses and men took part in many 'civilian and agricultural tasks'. Discipline within the newly formed unit was not all that it might have been, but we are led to believe that, by and large, relatively harmonious relations existed between the new occupants of St John's Wood Farm and their neighbours (which is still the case).

Volume II of the 'Regimental Companion' lists the following numbers on the strength of the Corps at that time:

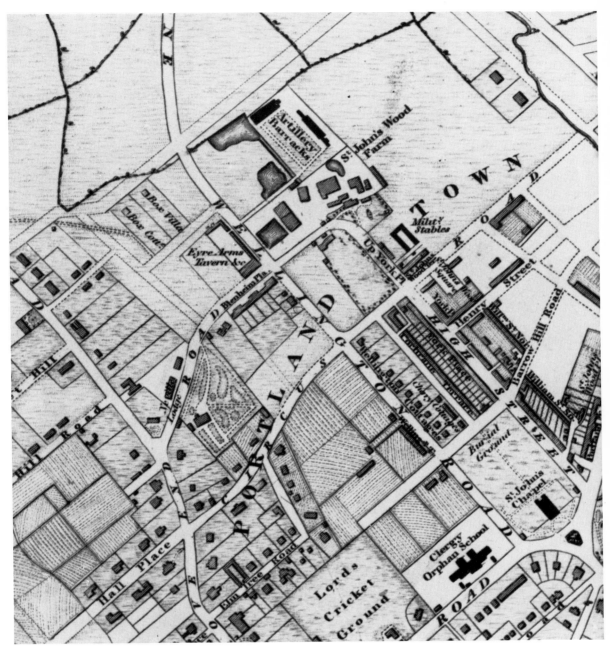

Map of St John's Wood, 1830. The 'military stables' to the south-east of the barracks are now residential culs-de-sacs where the 'boxes' are currently priced at about £350,000 each!

'One Lieut., a Sgt and 3 Corporals and about 45 Drivers and 90 horses (including riding horses) with a collar maker, wheeler and 2 shoeing smiths are attached to a heavy Brigade; and 1 Lieut., 2 Corporals and 38 Drivers and 75 horses with the same amount of Artificers to a Light Brigade'.

The neo-Georgian Officers' Mess, built in the early 1920s. The lamp above the doorway and the small wrought-iron fence were made in the forge.

By 1810 it had become quite evident that to have horses and guns so far apart was inconvenient and uneconomical. It was decided, despite protests by Thomas Willan, the Eyres' tenant, that more land and buildings were required at St John's Wood. A block of land just north of the farmyard was eventually secured and is the site of the present barracks. The 'New Artillery Barracks' were completed in 1812, and left much to be desired as far as both human and equine accommodation were concerned. However, horses, men and guns – smooth-bore muzzle-loading brass pieces – were all together at The Wood, and the foundations of today's barracks were well and truly laid.

This happy state of affairs was not to last long. At the end of the Napoleonic campaign it was (as is normally the case after a war) decided to run down the armed forces. In 1819 'in conse-quence of the peace' the Artillery Brigade was moved to Woolwich and unsuccessful efforts were made by the Board of Ordnance to get rid of the barracks. It was decided that, as artillery was now more mobile and could therefore be deployed more quickly, it was no longer necessary to billet artillery so close to the metropolis for anti-riot purposes ... 'the assistance of Artillery can always be had in a short time from Woolwich'. It would be wrong to suppose that London-based artillery was solely deployed for 'domestic' reasons. It is recorded in the *Observer* of February 1807, after the capture of Curaçao, that 'At one o'clock the Park and Tower guns announced this important acquisition'; probably the first salute to be fired from The Wood.

In 1824 work began on one of the King's Troop's most valuable assets – the Riding School. This magnificent structure, standing 184 feet 6 inches long and 64 feet 6 inches wide, was originally designed and built for the Cavalry Riding Establishment who were looking for a home. The 'Riding House' was completed in just nine months on 20 March 1825 at a cost of £5712 4s 9d. Compliments must be paid to Brevet Major Tylden of the Royal Engineers who designed the building. It has withstood the test of time extremely well, the only structural problem being three beams requiring 'damp rot' treatment in the autumn of 1982 – 157 years later! However, within five years of the school's completion the Cavalry Riding Establishment was moved to Maidstone and once again the barracks stood empty. It is interesting to note that despite the presence of the school and the occupation of mounted units within the barracks for some 20 odd years, stabling only existed for about 25 horses, the remainder being housed in Ordnance Mews, at the top of St John's Wood High Street.

In 1832 new tenants arrived at The Wood. This time it was the turn of the Recruit Depôt of Foot Guards who, like the Cavalry Riding Establishment, had lost their own barracks to 'improvements'. Their stay was to be the shortest so far – one year only. They were, however, followed by a succession of infantry battalions – who occupied the barracks off and on until 1876. They in turn were followed for the next four years by the Household Cavalry, while their own barracks at Knightsbridge were rebuilt. During this period the wooden stables were constructed to accommodate 'temporarily' 128 horses. These same stables were demolished in 1969 to make way for the new barracks.

Two ironical points emerge. The first is documented in Joan Wanklyn's wonderful account of the barracks in *Guns at the Wood*. While the Troop waited from 1969 to 1972 to have their new barracks completed they were in turn the guests of the Household Cavalry in Combermere Barracks at Windsor, ie the positions were exactly reversed! The other odd fact is that the 'temporary' wooden barracks lasted for 94 years though Knightsbridge had to undergo a second rebuild in less than 100 years.

The occupants of the Barracks are listed on a board outside the guardroom.

ST JOHN'S WOOD BARRACKS

1804	CORPS OF GUNNER DRIVERS
1819	BARRACKS VACATED
1822	CAVALRY RIDING ESTABLISHMENT
1835	GUARDS RECRUITS DEPOT
1836	VARIOUS DETACHMENTS OF FOOT GUARDS
1876	1st LIFE GUARDS
1880	A BATTERY A BRIGADE RHA
1881	G BATTERY C BRIGADE RHA
1883	C BATTERY A BRIGADE RHA
1886	B BATTERY B BRIGADE RHA
1888	B BATTERY A BRIGADE RHA
1889	J BATTERY RHA
1891	VACANT
1893	D BATTERY RHA
1896	G BATTERY RHA
1899	VACANT
1900	V BATTERY RHA
1902	X BATTERY RHA
1904	Y BATTERY RHA
1906	A BATTERY RHA
1908	B/B BATTERY RHA
1911	F BATTERY RHA
1914	VACANT
1915	B RESERVE BRIGADE RHA
1919	F BATTERY RHA
1920	N BATTERY RHA
1923	O BATTERY RHA
1926	M BATTERY RHA
1929	J BATTERY RHA
1932	F BATTERY RHA
1936	K BATTERY RHA
1939	LONDON DISTRICT SIGNAL TROOP
1946	THE RIDING TROOP RHA
1947	THE KINGS TROOP RHA
1969	BARRACKS VACATED FOR REBUILD
1972	THE KINGS TROOP RHA

The front entrance of Jubilee Buildings, on the west side of the barracks.

In 1880, the Household Cavalry moved out, and on 24 June, A Battery A Brigade, later the Chestnut Troop Royal Horse Artillery, moved into St John's Wood from Aldershot. It was undoubtedly a major turning point in the history of the barracks which finally appeared to have received its rightful tenants. Apart from lapses in the two World Wars, Horse Artillery have been there ever since.

During the tenure of the early RHA Batterys very little building or improvements took place, and they carried out much the same duties as we do today, in considerably less favourable circumstances. The wooden stables were quite adequate, so the horses lived in a fair degree of comfort – in stalls, of course, as they do to this day. The men, however, did not fare so well. They also lived in wooden huts with very little in the way of washing facilities or sanitation. The Riding School was used to house the guns as well as the stores and a harness room, so only half could be used for riding. Despite these and other inconveniences, successive Batteries performed their ceremonial tasks in a most impressive way. They took part over the years in all the great affairs of State, including the funeral of

King Edward VII in 1910 and the coronation of King George V the following year. The Musical Drive also figured prominently on their annual agenda.

In the years following the Great War the barracks were greatly improved. The Officers Mess, described as 'neo-Georgian', was completed in 1922. It has withstood the test of time in a most excellent manner, and has been the location for many of the great occasions at The Wood, not least of all the visit by King George VI. It has a most friendly atmosphere and is far more like a house than a Mess, while still able to cater admirably for all the officers and one or two visitors besides.

Also built in the 1920s was the Sergeants Mess which didn't match the officers' home in any shape or form. The cookhouse/dining hall, however, was of a high standard and definitely improved the lot of the soldiers who then, as now, worked hard for long hours and deserved to eat well and in decent surroundings. The washing and sanitary arrangements were also improved when ablution annexes were added to the barrack blocks. A forage and gun park were also completed at about this time.

In 1935 the married quarters, known as Jubilee Buildings, were opened. This five-storey building, which runs the width of the western end of the barracks, is of incalculable value; it allows The Wood to be as self-contained as any barracks can be. The soldiers are in the lines by 0600 daily and the close proximity of Jubilee Buildings ensures that this is no more of a chore than it need be. Initially it housed 68 families but when modernised in 1974 the figure was reduced to 56, including maisonettes on the top floor.

The last major chapter in The Wood's history began in the autumn of 1969, when the King's Troop left for Combermere Barracks in Windsor. Here the Troop lived for two and a half years while the old barracks (except the Officers Mess and the Riding School) were demolished. I've always been glad that I personally knew the old barracks, even though very briefly, thanks to that great Horse Gunner, the late Brigadier JC Friedberger. In the few days I had to spare between leaving Ireland and joining Mons OCS, he organised a tour of the mounted units for me. I only spent 76 hours at The Wood but it was enough time to explore most of the nooks and crannies and to get the 'feel' of The 'old' Wood and its very special atmosphere.

During the Troop's stay at Combermere we enjoyed excellent relations with our hosts, the 'mechanised' regiments of the Household Cavalry – the Life Guards and The Blues and Royals. The Troop Captain during our sojourn there was Captain Humphrey Mews who now, as Colonel, is Chairman of the Gunner Saddle Club. He spent a lot of his time scurrying back

The guardroom today is exactly opposite the spot where the old one stood.

to The Wood advising the architect and builders in turn as to our requirements. He personally monitored the rebuild, and is largely responsible for the standard which was achieved.

The Troop meanwhile perfected the firing of salutes in London from Windsor. We used to box up at 0600 on the squares at Combermere and proceed in convoy to Regent's Park barracks. Here the horses would be stabled in the vehicle 'garages', which were converted stables and conveniently still had rings on the walls. After we had breakfasted, the soldiers would set to for stables parade followed by 'Boot and Saddle' and 'File Out'. We trotted to Hyde Park via the Marylebone Road and halted in the traditional place, Bryanston Square, before heading off for the Saluting Base. It didn't take long for us to 'fine tune' the post salute drills, and as often as not the horses would be back in their Windsor stalls by a quarter past two.

After three years away, the spring of 1972 finally heralded the Troop's return to a brand new custom-built barracks. On 17 April, having unboxed as usual at Regent's Park Barracks, the Troop marched joyfully back to The 'new' Wood to be greeted by Major-General Bowes-Lyon CB, OBE, MC, Commanding The Household Division and London District. Despite our very pleasant exile at Windsor it was a wonderful feeling to come home and to have the Troop back where it truly belonged. I shall never forget the long pause during the candlelit dinner in the Officers Mess that night when the sounds of the Last Post died away across the brand-new square – it was a very nostalgic moment.

The new barracks are a great success. The stables are first-class, with the Troop horses living in roomy stalls (11 foot × 6 foot) complete with automatic watering systems. They are separated by creosoted railway sleepers and can be broken down into loose boxes if required. Each section of approximately 34 horses has its own sub section offices, forage area and upstairs harness room in an adjoining building. In a separate part of the barracks, the chargers are stabled in spacious loose boxes which also have adjacent tack and forage rooms. The soldiers are also well housed in comfortable rooms on the three floors above the gun park. Soldiers from The Wood of yester-year would envy their modern ablutions and airy rooms, not to mention an up-to-date NAAFI and dining room complete with fruit machine.

The Sergeants at long last have the Mess they so rightly deserve. Tucked away in the south-east corner of the barracks, beyond a well-kept lawn, it has been lovingly added to in the 12 years since its completion. Its walls drip with brasses, bronzes, silver and pictures, mostly depicting the exploits of previous generations. In the well-known (though not so well

The charger lines house the officers' horses in considerable comfort.

The Senior NCOs were finally given the mess that they deserved in the '69–'72 rebuild.

documented) traditions of the Horse Artillery, many a young officer has 'lost his name' within its four walls already!

The rest of the buildings boast most of the amenities required of a modern barracks plus a number of features basic to the needs of training horses. The Riding School, returned to its former size, is well capable of hosting a jumping competition, dressage display or two concurrent rides, while the slightly smaller 'all weather' manège with its floodlights, can absorb the remaining activities. An additional 'all weather' track circumventing the square allows the Troop to exercise should the frost prevent venturing out on to the streets. The headquarters block, 'Q' stores, education and medical rooms all prove very adequate for their jobs, and the forge, extended slightly since 1972, is one of the finest in the country.

So despite one or two minor problems The 'new' Wood is a fitting home for the horses and men who live there. As the years go by and it looks more and more 'lived in', it is earning the title of 'Home'.

CHAPTER FOUR

Establishment

THE TROOP, in keeping with other military units, is periodically under scrutiny with a view to making us more cost effective. This in turn occasionally results in some trimming of manpower, but we are, however, still 'one of the most complete things in the army'. The Duke of Richmond would have been well pleased to see that so long after he fashioned A Troop at his home in Sussex such a model still exists, though modified in some aspects. The barracks are designed to house the three sections, each divided into two subsections responsible for providing one complete gun team. The sections are commanded by Subalterns, or Captains, who in turn have a Sergeant in charge of each subsection. The Number One, as he is known, has a Bombardier and two Lance Bombardiers to assist him in the day to day running of his sub – probably 17 horses and about as many gunners.

A Number One has to allocate his men to a variety of tasks within his own sub, not to mention the various Troop fatigues that constantly call for manpower.

Each sub has its own limber gunner whose duty it is to maintain his 13-pounder QF gun in a working and immaculate condition.

The Troop has ten 13-pounders altogether, all of which fired in the Great War and half of which were used (believe it or not) in an anti-aircraft role during World War II. The gun owes its origins to the 'Horse and Field Gun Committee' which was convened as the South African war drew to a close, to draw up specifications for two new guns. The result, which became the main Horse Artillery armament for the Great War, incorporated an Armstrong wire-wound gun, a Vickers recoil system, and a carriage designed by the Royal Carriage Department of Woolwich. The 13-pounder was specifically designed for Royal Horse Artillery and, like its big brother the 18-pounder, came into production in 1904. They are ideal ceremonial guns, with large areas of brass and chrome to catch the sun or the spotlights, and equally huge expanses of leather to be 'bliffed' to eternity. Add to this the white rope-covering on the recoil system and the snowy-white drag ropes on the shield, and you have a lot

'F' Sub – the Blacks, whose particular job is to take part in state and high-ranking military funerals. For this duty they must always have a number of steady horses on hand, which is not a simple matter when they are full of corn at the height of the show season. Neither is it easy these days to find black horses.

of cleaning and polishing to do. As there are no spares they are also used in practice, devoid of their 'whites' and dressed in 'elephant covers'.

The limber gunners are led by an Artificer Staff Sergeant, or 'Tiffy' as they've been affectionately known over the years. These dedicated men from the Royal Electrical and Mechanical Engineers are a vital cog in the Troop wheel. The guns, although weighing (with their limbers) one and half tons, are clearly not in their first flush of youth and need a 'nanny' of immense enthusiasm and skill. This requirement has always been fulfilled; generations of 'Tiffies' have nursed, rebuilt and touched up the Troop guns to keep them in an immaculate condition. Without the dedication of these men from another Corps the Troop would soon grind to a halt.

Harness cleaners are also an integral part of a subsection. Although all the drivers 'turn in' to rift out the forged steel of the 'bottom' or working harness, it is just one man (unless time is tight) who is responsible for the 'top' or parade harness. The art of 'bliffing' (spit and polish) is fast dying out in the rest of the Army, but we, like other members of the Household Troops, are regular exponents of this difficult art. During the

Show Season especially, a top-harness cleaner will have a permanent stain on his fingers as layer after layer of boot polish is applied in a magical way until every item of the harness from breast collar to galloping-strap gleams like glass.

The duties of the men in a subsection – where every soldier in the Troop begins his career – are varied, and involve a lot of hard work. Apart from mucking out and riding exercise which take place every morning – when there isn't a draught parade or performance – he must clean or bliff the saddles and head-collars, sweep the yard, tidy the muck heap, press his uniforms and of course groom his horses until they shine. Most accept the graft willingly because they love their horses. Others take on a special role within the stables and become 'stablemen', responsible for making up the feeds and watching over the horses when everyone else is otherwise engaged. Even a youth-ful and relatively inexperienced stableman is an asset not to be wasted when commanding a section. By tradition a rather scruffy individual in his denims and 'bush jacket', he will be the first to notice that 'Fanny is off her feed' or '32 has got a lump on his knee'.

In addition to those working permanently in his lines, the Number One will also have on his strength some trumpeters (who always have a practice just as they are needed in the lines), and grooms who look after the officers' chargers. In fact a large proportion of his paper strength is permanently missing – which generally results in one man doing two horses in addition to his other tasks.

The King's Troop is administered by Troop Headquarters, which is made up of the CO, Adjutant and RSM, ably supported by a Chief Clerk and his office staff. Soldiers who work for the various internal services such as the Saddlers or Farriers are known as the Staff Employed. They are headed by the Troop Captain, who with the close assistance of the RQMS and BQMS is responsible for maintaining all the services required to keep the Troop on the road. In fact the Captain's empire covers a multitude of duties from making all the entries for over 100 competitions a year to ensuring that the radiators in Lance-Bombardier Bloggs' flat are working; he is seldom idle. In addition to these domestic items he also has the entrepreneurial task of finding good shows for the Troop to perform at and a sponsor to help bear the ever increasing costs.

The Staff Employed include the tradesmen, among whom are six farriers who work in the most modern of forges. They have their own hierarchical structure, with a Master Farrier of Staff Sergeant rank, a Sergeant, a Bombardier, and a number of Gunner apprentices under constant supervision. The Army School of Farriery is an integral part of the Royal Army Veterinary Corps Depôt at Melton Mowbray, and King's Troop

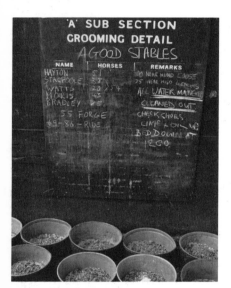

Stable noticeboard. The Junior NCO-in-charge allocates the tasks.

Hot shoeing. A qualified farrier perfects
the fit of a shoe, while an apprentice looks
on.

A 'D' Sub soldier oils up the hooves of
Sequin.

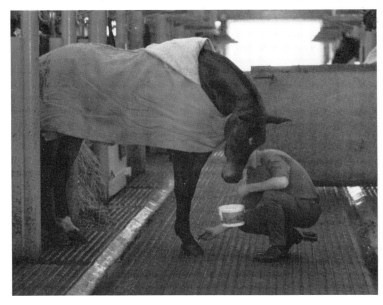

(Above) The Master Tailor and his assistant adjust the new RSM's No 2 Dress Jacket to the Troop pattern. (Left) 'Tiffy' replacing a brake-pad in his workshop. He is constantly 'nannying' the guns and making little alterations to keep them on the road. (Opposite, top) In the Bottom Harness Room saddles are being prepared and harness assembled. (Right) A standard military saddle, blanket and surcingle; and a Driver's whip.

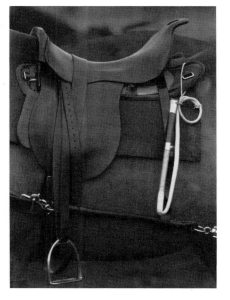

farriers regularly go there for upgrading courses. During the autumn there is also one away with the remounts at Larkhill. Farriery within the Army is a very specialised trade, and standards must be kept at a high level. Military farriers only take two and a half years to train, as opposed to four in 'civvy street', and in addition they are qualified veterinary 'dressers'. It is therefore all the more important that quality control is maintained both at the RAVC Depôt and also within the mounted units. Staff Sergeant Morgan, who recently retired as Master Farrier after 22 years' service with the Troop, has also been farrier to the British International Three-Day Event Team since 1970.

The Troop also boasts its own tailor's shop, again headed by a Staff Sergeant with a staff of two. During the Training Season they are kept busy fitting every soldier in the barracks into his Number 2 Dress or Full Dress, depending on his job; most soldiers have both. The Horse Artillery drill of mounting and dismounting on the move ensures that they perfect the art of sewing on buttons – hundreds of 'em! The presiding Master Tailor is also responsible for ensuring that the Troop is up to date on Nuclear, Biological and Chemical Warfare as well as its Battle Fitness Tests – a versatile NCO to be sure.

Although all the harness, saddles and leatherwork generally

(Left) A Driver's leg-iron, which protects him from the traces or draught pole. (Above) The two centre-sets of A Sub's bottom harness and a headcollar are carried to the harness room ready to be stripped and cleaned.

are issued from Ordnance, some of them are over 50 years old. They can all be repaired, or even made, if necessary, in our own saddlers' shop. The Master Saddler, or 'Waxy' as these craftsmen have long been known, presides over three saddlers in a tiny little shop beside the Top Harness Room. Among the rolls of leather, riding boots, and half-finished saddles, can be found the latest equipment required for the saddler's trade. Saddlers all qualify within the army system, as well as achieving the various civilian diplomas to the highest level of proficiency. It is important for these men to be highly skilled in the art of making and repairing harness, as broken traces or faulty couplings seriously undermine the confidence of the drivers whose lives may depend on them. One of the severest tests of their skills is to render safe an incoming officer's personal tack which – probably made in India before the last War – has lain in a musty trunk for a generation!

We also have a small veterinary team consisting of a veterinary officer and his NCO assistant who carry out a 2- or 3-year tour with the Troop. Between them they are responsible for all the horse documentation as well as the usual day to day complaints found in a large stable of working horses. The VO's first job is to gain the confidence of all ranks by a clear demonstration of

Before File Out the Limber Gunners push the 1½-ton gun and limber out on to the square for the teams to 'hook-in'. The guns look deceptively light as they run easily across the tarmac – but it is a different story in deep mud. The covers are kept on whenever possible to protect the guns from damage.

his professional skills. Most 'horsey' people – and soldiers are no exception – think that they know better than vets. Unless the VO can quickly demonstrate his competence, the lines soon produce their own experts, sometimes with disastrous results. By and large, over the years the Troop has been most fortunate in its veterinary personnel, and receives an excellent service, especially in times of crisis.

The rest of the Staff Employed who make up the complement of the 187 All Ranks are cooks, who produce equally excellent food in or out of barracks, and the MT drivers who keep the Troop's small fleet of lorries, Land Rovers and horse boxes on the road.

CHAPTER FIVE

Training

ONE OF THE MANY JOYS of life in the Troop is that things don't change very much. The annual calendar follows a time-honoured format which can sometimes be added to (but rarely subtracted from) if a trip abroad materialises in the winter. The programme for any one year is 90 per cent organised by mid-summer the preceding year, which means that all ranks are aware of what is going on and when; this in turn allows soldiers to plan their own private lives well in advance.

The year starts when Christmas leave is over in mid-January. Leave in the Troop differs from that of a mechanised unit (ie the rest of the Army) in that any regiment lucky enough to take block leave is able to close the garage doors, lock up its vehicles, and go home. Obviously the Troop cannot do that, so a double system of leave has to be arranged. In other words, half the soldiers go on leave while the other half 'double up' until 'changeover' day when the first leave returns and the remainder go away. Over the Christmas/New Year period this works well, as the horses are 'let down' to only one hour's exercise a day and life is relatively quiet by Troop standards. We try to organise the changeover two days after Boxing Day, allowing the officers and senior ranks to serve the soldiers their Christmas lunch – preceded of course by that favourite of all trumpet calls, 'Christmas Dinner', sounded by every trumpeter in the Troop.

When leave is over, emphasis is placed upon returning to normal as quickly as possible. Horses and men (though, it is hoped, not harness) are all a bit rusty and need to be sharpened up. In the last couple of weeks of leave, those at work will have started trimming and re-clipping, while the bottom harness will have been rifted and polished ready for the first draught parade. The period from mid-January to the end of February is given over to Section Training and is very much at the Section Commander's disposal. During this time he must ensure that his men and horses are ready to join the other two sections as a cohesive Troop to take part in the year's ceremonial ahead. In addition to this rather grand and general objective, he must also ensure that a multitude of other necessary chores take

The first stages of breaking-in a remount to draught work.

February: the early days of section training. Note the horse's fat tummy! Galloping fitness is achieved by mid-April, in time for the show season.

The Centre Driver's job is to keep the traces up and to maintain a continuous line of draught. Slack traces result in the team 'snatching' or – worse still – a 'leg-over', which is the most common cause of a stoppage in the Drive.

'Eyes Left'. The Drivers' whips go across the collar pads of the Hand horses to keep them in draught during the March Past.

On the square at the Wood the Hand Wheeler of 'A' Sub practises a new technique of breeching! The Wheelers are the hardest-working horses in the team. They pull like all the others but are the only ones who have to stop the guns.

'Dismount'. Like everything else in the Troop, this is performed as a drill.

place. His men must have lectures on everything from Queen's Regulations to drugs and insurance; they must have their Full Dress and Number Two dress correctly fitted; and remounts must continue their draught training. It is a busy period for all, with a Royal Salute thrown in to keep everyone on their toes.

The Salute in question is fired on the anniversary of Her Majesty's Accession to the Throne – 6 February. Of all the salutes that we fire this is the one that concerns me – and I suspect concerned my predecessors – most. It is the first one of the year, coming quite soon after work has resumed, and a lot of the jobs are being done by new personnel for the first time. The weather at this time of year is normally rather unpleasant, and Hyde Park, especially over the underground car park, is very wet and even boggy in places.

However much the Troop practises this Salute (generally two or three times) there is always a risk, as with most of the Troop's parades, that something can go wrong. If the mechanics of a Salute are examined, it can easily be seen what enormous scope for error exists. Seventy-one horses and 53 men come into line at the north end of the Park and then gallop across the grass and zig-zagging paths to the Saluting Base; 36 of these horses, divided into six teams, have a ton-and-a-half of gun and limber behind them. On arrival, the 'detachments' or men who fire the gun must dismount at the canter and bring the piece 'into action' in double quick time, while the limbers and 'empty horses' return to the 'wagon lines' as fast as they came. Twenty-three horses in all require to be led on the return journey. A sigh of relief can be heard all round as the first one-pound charge detonates on the dot of noon.

When the Accession Salute is over, Section Training gets under way again. From my office window I can watch the

A draught parade. 'Form Column of Route, 'D' Sub leading – Walk – March.' The Troop is on its way to the Training Ground, Old Oak Common at the western end of Wormwood Scrubs.

progress of men and horses – recalcitrant wheelers with the breeching on for the first time, or a Section Commander encouraging his new charger to accept Sword Drill.

The Troop's training area is at Wormwood Scrubs, which lies a few miles (or an hour's hack) due west of St John's Wood. Here, beside the famous prison, lies 181 acres of grass which was made available for military use by an Act of Parliament in 1897. In 1980 the area was restricted to 65 acres which prevents much manoeuvering as a Troop, but still allows us to practise the Drive and Royal Salutes.

Two mornings a week the sections file out of the barrack gates en route for the Scrubs or Regent's Park to introduce remounts to the gun teams or older horses into new positions. With luck the drivers will not have changed too much since the previous season; and the introduction can go quite swiftly – although the centre driver is often new, as his predecessor will have progressed to the wheel position. It is a very rewarding time for a Section Commander as he trains his section – 34 horses or more, plus about the same number of men. It is his opportunity to mould them to his satisfaction for the demands that lie ahead.

The only other form of training carried on at this time is Mobilisation Training, whereby the Troop, or half at a time, goes away to a Training Area for five days' 'soldiering'. The Troop has always lived gloriously in the past and studiously avoided 'playing soldiers' at any price. However, nowadays as the Army gets smaller and each unit must be more cost effective (and must be seen to be), the Troop is moving with the times. We must play our part and take our place within London District and the other Household Troops as reliable trained soldiers. Each man on joining the Troop will have passed out of 'basic training' (16 weeks) at the Royal Artillery Training Regiment at the Depôt in Woolwich, or even longer with the Junior Leaders Regiment, Royal Artillery, at Bramcote, so he should have the basic skills required of a recruit. A few soldiers come to the Troop from 'service' regiments and they tend to be the mainstay of Mobilisation Training among the rank and file, while our own 'homegrown' senior NCOs act as instructors, having been away on courses to acquire the necessary skills. We are fortunate to have visiting NCOs from the Guards battalions who assist the home team and add the necessary realism to our training.

This military training is on the increase and so is the Troop's proficiency. More and more periods are allocated to weapon training and infantry drills so that the lead driver of a galloping gun team can swap his gold braid and busby for 'combats' and

During Mobilisation Training the Troop moves out of barracks to a training area in order to practise infantry drills for its mobilisation role.

a beret, his driver's whip for a rifle and can lead his section on a night patrol or whatever else may be demanded of him. Needless to say, 'a change is as good as a rest' and enthusiasm among all ranks abounds.

During Section Training the officers squeeze in their last few days hunting in Leicestershire and take part in that wonderful sporting contest, the Melton Ride. This splendid event, which harks back to the old-fashioned point-to-point, is an annual occasion in the Leicestershire calendar and is keenly contested by Meltonians and outsiders alike. The event is run over three and a half miles of natural hunting country with as few turning places as possible. Those Troop horses that spend their winter at the Royal Army Vetinary Corps Depôt at Melton Mowbray are pitted against those of the Household Cavalry and Foot Guards in competition for the soldiers' prize, 'Best Soldier on an Army Horse'. I remember my own excitement when 'Toofy' (Number 18 from B Sub) won it for me in 1973, having been passed by the CO on 'Jet' no fewer than three times – he either had three falls or his map reading was seriously at fault. A few years before, Captain Bill Thatcher won the race outright on his own horse, Sun Ray, a notable achievement by any standards.

Annual Administrative Inspection. The Major-General inspects Left Section before the Troop moves off to walk, trot and gallop past the Saluting Base.

By the last week of February, all the horses have returned from 'Winter Training' at Melton, and Troop Training begins. This is the time that the Troop must get its act together before the 'Show Season' begins, traditionally in early May at the Royal Windsor Horse Show. During this two-month period there is usually a State Visit either at Windsor or in London, a Salute to be fired for the anniversary of the Queen's 'proper' birthday (21 April), with perhaps a 'funny' of some description thrown in for good measure. At this time of year there are also two other parades which are arguably the most exciting to carry out and impressive to watch: the Major General's Annual Inspection and the dress rehearsal, carried out in front of the Director Royal Artillery, a few days earlier.

This Annual Inspection, known as the 'Gallop Past', is a severe test of the Troop's skills, and it embodies all the glorious pageantry of the old days. The Major-General Commanding London District and The Household Division rides on to the side of the parade ground, escorted by his staff officers, the Troop Adjutant and the Veterinary Officer, to the accompaniment of the Royal Artillery Band, Woolwich. The latter will have visited The Wood at least three times to re-familiarise the horses with their music! After inspecting the Troop, the Major-

The Troop Point-to-Point at Kimble in Buckinghamshire. Only the 'gun pullers' compete now, as the chargers used to set too fast a pace, turning the race into a procession.

General, resplendent in cocked hat bedecked with swan feathers, gives permission to 'carry on', which sets the Troop in motion. In the confined corner of Regent's Park allotted to us, the Troop manoeuvres about in open and close interval to walk past, trot past, and eventually, shoulder to shoulder, at the gallop.

Needless to say the event is not always without incident. During my first rehearsal as CO, I witnessed an officer, who had been bucked off, producing Olympic speed in his (successful) effort to avoid a 'wall' of galloping horses and swinging guns. This demonstration of speed and agility (by one not normally known for such qualities) took place at Wormwood Scrubs. Captain G R Prest – who was then Left Section Commander – hit the ground, complete with sword, about 30 yards in front of his section just as I had signalled the gallop. I turned round (having heard the thud) in time to see the diminutive Prest, sword in hand, diving out of the way of F Sub, the Blacks. A shaken and white-faced officer was heard to say 'they weren't going to stop.' . . . 'Stop?' cried his lead driver, 'we was aiming at yer, Sir!' Happily it is possible to report that the parade itself went without a hitch.

During this time of the year a number of sporting occasions figure prominently in the Troop calendar. Within barracks

Remount training at Larkhill. 'Backing one for the first time'. It doesn't always work out quite as the book says it should! (Note that since these photographs were taken the army has introduced a rule that hard hats must be worn during remount training.)

there is the 'Sounding Competion' in which all the trumpeters take part. The Troop works religiously to the trumpet in barracks, the first call, 'Reveille', being sounded at 0600 hours throughout the year, the final call being 'Last Post' at 2200 hours. The trumpeters, all ex 'boys' from the Junior Leaders Regiment, practise hard to achieve a high standard for daily sounding, let alone the competition. A 'bum note' from a 'chunky' (recruit) is greeted with howls of derision from all over the barracks – a succession of them could lead to the muck heap via a watertrough.

Also in the spring the Troop holds a dressage competition in the manège behind the Guard Room. As with the Sounding Competition, guest judges are invited to mark the various tests, and it is usually (unlike most dressage) an afternoon of amusing entertainment as the 'Fifteen Bobbers' demonstrate their dislike of discipline to the delight of the onlookers. Actually the standard has improved enormously over the years and some good tests have been produced in Riding Club and British Horse Society events. We run our own One-Day Event in March or April at either Bucklebury in Berkshire or Tweseldown near Aldershot. It is an excellent day out for all ranks and their wives, with a very good lunch laid on for everyone. The

'hairies' dislike of discipline in general, and dressage in particular, is made up for by their enthusiasm for going as fast as possible in wide open spaces, and most competitors experience an exhilarating cross-country ride.

The Troop Point-to-Point takes place in April and is another splendid day out. We share the meeting with that august body of legal equestrians, the Pegasus Club. Their members ride at The Wood throughout the winter and the point-to-point is a culmination of our winter association, the Troop traditionally having the last race on the card. The conditions have changed over the years, and I believe the current format, arrived at by one of my predecessors, is the right one. The race is only open to lines horses, and private horses or chargers may not take part; there is no qualifications for jockeys other than that they must be members of the Troop. When I won it in 1971 on my charger, Miss Wrigglesworth, the lines horses were galloped off their legs by some high quality chargers and only a few finished. Now, with 'gun-pullers' only, going at a sensible pace (under strict orders and dire threats), the race is a good one. It is also not without amusement, and in my year I was beaten to the first fence by both trumpeters who had heralded the start of the contest. It is also a good betting medium, as a dozen

Recruits Ride. The recruits spend a lot of time going down the grid with arms folded, singing out their name, rank, and number.

hogged-mane 'hairies' with blanks in the breeding column on the racecard cause a jittery market among those bookies brave enough to stay. Fortunately for them, sentimental money and section pride cut their losses.

The Troop also plays its part in the Regimental meeting at Sandown. For the centenary year we provided mounted trumpeters to lead the runners out on to the course and back in to the winner's enclosure before heralding the prize-giving with a fanfare. Also on parade were two guns for the young to gawp at and the old and bold to criticise. The meeting was a great success – being won by no other than Captain Prest of 'Gallop Past' fame on his and Lieutenant-Colonel Deacon's 'De Pluvinel'. The Troop also owns its own steeplechaser, Monkswell, which having trained partly at Larkhill with the regimental racehorse, Colonial Lad, won a Hunter 'Chase at Towcester in the new Troop colours (royal blue with a yellow hoop and blue and yellow checked cap).

Troop training ends with a gunnery day for the officers at Larkhill on Salisbury Plain. They go down the night before for an indoor session at the School of Artillery with an Instructor in Gunnery, who puts them through their paces on Invertron. This wonderful invention simulates shoots on a projected screen, allowing students to blaze away with mythical shells at little or no cost to the tax payer. After a couple of hours of Fireplanning, the officers repair to a local hostelry to fortify themselves for the 'real thing' next morning. Despite the day's training being most enjoyable, officers are expected to hit the target given to them – and rapidly, too. In 1970 when I joined the Troop as a Section Commander there was a slightly different approach to the day's sport. Breeches and boots were 'de rigeur', vintage port was much in evidence and the Veterinary Officer, shooting for the first time, corrected his opening round with a cry of 'Right, three furlongs!'. Nowadays, in keeping with the Troop's effort to be professional in the field, as well as on parade, a somewhat more serious approach is taken; however, I am happy to say that 'lunch in the field' is every bit as good as it used to be. The day was summed up nicely by a senior officer when he described the activities as 'relaxed excellence'.

And so, after a multitude of lectures, gun drill, Mobilisation Training, competitions and rides, the Troop is ready to begin the Show Season in the second week of May. There have probably been something in the order of 20 draught parade days days at the Scrubs, before the Windsor Show. A standard draught parade is very hard work for the horses, involving the hour's hack to the Scrubs, maybe two or even three Musical Drive practices down there plus an hour's return journey – in all, four hours out of barracks; the horses are pretty fit, therefore, by the time Royal Windsor approaches. The 'proof of the pudding is in the eating' and the first Musical Drive of the year, under floodlights and before Her Majesty, is a tense occasion for all ranks.

CHAPTER SIX

The Show Season: May to July

THE ROYAL WINDSOR HORSE SHOW is one of the Troop's favourites. Despite the natural nervousness of the season's first Drive, all ranks enjoy the week, especially if the weather is good which sadly isn't often the case. The dwindling number of personnel who served at Windsor during the 'rebuild' always enjoy moving back into Combermere barracks and boring their juniors with tales of 'the old days'. As elements of the Household Cavalry Regiment are likely to be in residence, equine accommodation is usually a bit cramped, and some horses are picqueted in the Riding School. However, from now on – thanks to an interest-free loan of £25,000 from the Worshipful Company of Saddlers – none of the horses will be on heel lines or in a position to bite and kick each other. The Troop has acquired 84 mobile stalls which will accommodate the horses in comfort and safety within the school and under canvas at the shows.

Soldiers are housed in one of the resident regiment's barrack blocks, and for the first few evenings after arrival they have time to wander around the beautiful 'Royal' town. There is also plenty of opportunity for soldiers to see a bit of the Show and even to take part if so inclined. The Troop normally fields a large entry for the show-jumping competitions (especially for the Queen's Cup) and the tent-pegging class.

The Drive itself, on the Saturday night, is set off by the backdrop of the floodlit castle and is usually a good one. Horses will have been introduced to the arena and its floodlights the night before, and strict instructions are issued to those personnel not on parade to ensure that the exit is kept clear for the 'gallop out'. In the early 1960s a woman dashed across the collecting ring as the teams were making their exit at full gallop. The leaders swerved to avoid her, and in so doing hit a tree. Two horses were subsequently destroyed, a lot of men were hurt, and the gun ended up on Old Windsor Road; the tree has since been removed.

Fortunately, however, such accidents are rare and tragic lessons such as that one have led to a tightening up of safety precautions and emergency drills all round. During the Drive,

RHA horses are a tough breed and bounce back from the most incredible entanglements. The horse in this photograph was up and away within moments.

be it at Windsor or any of the other big shows, a crash party of limber gunners in distinctive blue workmanlike 'fatigues' is always standing by, as are the veterinary officer, a horsebox and an ambulance. The officer in charge of the Drive (or Display as the 'outside' Drive is known) is responsible for initiating the various emergency drills once a mistake has been made. This he does by blowing his whistle to stop the performance and indicating, by a series of coloured flags, what action should be taken; no one may enter the arena until the whistle blows. Normally it is a simple 'leg-over' whereby a trace, usually on a tight turn, gets inside a horse's leg and has to be put back again by one of the leg-over parties stationed at each corner of the ring. Very often the most awful-looking accident results in no more than a graze. I remember at Windsor in 1971 a centre falling over in the traces and going the full length of

65

The Display

A sequence of photographs depicting the Display (as opposed to the Drive which is gun teams only) taken throughout the summer show season of 1984.

1. (Above) Guildford. The RSM, accompanied by the Provost Bombardier, inspects the trumpeters and markers. The trumpeters begin the display with a fanfare; the markers form an area which is the same size as the Earl's Court arena. The gun teams, devoid of Number One and detachments, perform a reduced Royal Tournament Drive culminating in the Scissors and Half-Battery Charge.

2. (Above) Putney. Two Section Commanders lead the Troop into the arena after the Parade Commander's trumpeter has sounded the 'Charge'. As they enter, the band strikes up 'Bonnie Dundee'.

3. (Above opposite) Aldershot. 'B' Subsection starting the 'Big Scissors'. The Troop splits into two half-batteries each one led by a Section Commander, criss-crosses the arena at the gallop.

4. (Right) Putney. The Wagon Wheel. The three Section Commanders and their trumpeters revolve around the Parade Commander. The detachments wheel around outside them, while the teams form the outer ring of the circle. The band appropriately plays 'Round the Marble Arch'. Putney Hospital forms the backdrop – very handy if the drivers miss their jerk'.

5. (Below opposite) Putney. 'B' Sub galloping round the arena to begin the Small Drive. The markers can be seen in the background, setting off to form the Small Drive arena.

6. (Right) Royal Show. The Scissors. Both teams are at full stretch as they cross each other. Timing is critical if the 60-foot-long gun teams are to maintain the 'flow' of this movement at the gallop.

7. (Bottom) Royal Show. Half-Battery Charge. After the Small Drive the guns pass through each other at the canter before forming up for the 'March Past'.

Continued on page 70

Only one foot on the ground between them as Willoughby and Solo 'coast' – a rare moment when the Wheelers are neither pulling nor breaking.

the wet arena on her back before the wheelers could stop the gun. She then stood up, shook herself and was put quickly back into the traces for the remainder of the Display; the recovery taking only a few seconds. As in so many 'show biz' – type accidents, the speed with which problems are rectified can save the show – we have even been accused of deliberate stoppages so that we can show off how quickly we can get started again!

After Windsor, the Troop is 'on the road' for the rest of May, performing at possibly three more shows before the first Salute in June – the anniversary of the Coronation.

It has always fascinated me watching the Troop leave for a show. All the packing is done during the two days before departure with the subsection 'coverer' (a bombardier, who is second in command of a sub) supervising the packing of the many different items of stable equipment. This multifarious assortment of equine militaria is carefully loaded into home-made boxes which open up into harness racks on arrival. A huge articulated container-lorry arrives the day before we leave, and into it go all the uniforms, harness, boxes and stable paraphernalia required to sustain the Troop in the field. The guns and limbers meanwhile are lovingly loaded by the limber gunners on to a custom-built two-tier lorry similar to those used for transporting cars; it is quite an education to watch the valuable guns being nosed up the steel ramp with one of the Land Rovers. Eventually, by the night before departure, every-

Witchcraft, 'B' Sub Number One's remount, begins to lose pace as they head for the Big Scissors at the Surrey County Show, Guildford.

thing is carefully accounted for and packed with only the horses – now well aware that something is afoot – still to be loaded.

At the prescribed time the following day as many as a dozen horseboxes turn up on the square to be designated to each subsection by the MT NCO. Within minutes of the first horse stepping up a ramp, what was a noisy barracks that has been bustling with activity since dawn or earlier, becomes a ghost town, with only a handful of horses and men remaining. These horses are mainly remounts, not yet safe enough to be exposed to a public performance, and their minders are probably in the same category! In these troubled times it is also necessary to leave a sizeable guard (plus dogs) to look after the security of the barracks. When we go on tour it takes nearly every man in the Troop to keep the show on the road and each one must know his job well and be confident that he can do it perfectly so as not to let down the rest of his team. Once performances get under way, the normal 11-hour working day of barrack life will probably stretch to 17 or more.

Two or three days before the horses leave, an advance party under the guidance of the Regimental Quarter-Master Sergeant will have arrived on site to set up the tented village which the Troop will occupy. If they do their job well and the lines are carefully set out, with water and electricity readily available, life is made comparatively simple, dependent on the vagaries of the weather. Each show is different from the last, but we

The Display *(continued from page 67)*

8. (Above) Royal Show. The March Past. The Troop marches past the Saluting Base. At the Royal Windsor Show the Salute is generally taken by Her Majesty The Queen.

10. (Left) Royal Show. The Commanding Officer, Equitation Instructor and Flag Man. If a mishap occurs, the CO is responsible for stopping the Display and organising the 'recovery'. This is done through a series of coloured flags or signals, each one of which signifies a set of actions to be taken by any one or all of the various emergency parties stationed around the arena. A horse-box and ambulance with engines running are always on hand just outside the ropes. The VO, a crash party, and two-man 'leg-over' parties are stationed inside the arena at strategic points.

11. (Above) Aldershot. 'Coming Into Action'. The guns are dropped into action at the gallop and they fire a one-pound charge individually (Battery Right) before firing a salvo. At Earl's Court only a 2oz charge has been allowed since pieces started dropping off the ceiling!

70

9. (Above) Guildford. A Section Commander leads his section into action.

---

12. (Left) Aldershot. The 'leg-over' party re-tie a broken loin strap.

13. (Below) Putney. The Gallop Out. Even if the Drive has produced problems, a good Gallop Out can save the day. As the teams emerge from the drifting smoke of the guns, led by the Parade Commander, the band once again plays the stirring canter tune 'Bonnie Dundee'. The horses strain into their breastcollars and the Drivers crouch down low over their necks with their whips urging on the hand horses; the music increases in tempo as the teams leave the arena at a flat-out gallop.

'A' Sub disappear into the smoke to pick up their gun. On a damp day the dense smoke often hangs about, reducing visibility to nil. It can be quite alarming for a Section Commander waiting around in the smoke for the teams to arrive; he can hear them coming towards him at full tilt but can't see them.

work to a standard format, and adapt it as and when required. If possible, 'civvy' marquees are used in preference to army tents as they give men and horses more living and working space. The horses live side-by-side under this huge expanse of canvas, while the men are usually accommodated in local barracks. Smaller tents are used for the gun park, offices, forage and stores. Throughout the show a duty officer lives on site and is responsible for the general welfare of the camp and all its inmates.

The month of June is always a busy one with the first fortnight or so being particularly hectic. As soon as the Troop arrives back in barracks from the last show in May it is time to practise a Salute, our most important task. The Coronation Salute is a standard one in that it is fired from the Royal Saluting Base in Hyde Park and therefore must be allotted 41 'bangs'; elsewhere in the country, except from the Tower of London, only 21 guns may be fired. No sooner is that Salute over than preparation begins for the June State Visit. The rehearsal usually takes place at the crack of dawn to ensure minimum disruption to the capital's traffic. This rehearsal takes place in khaki number 2 dress, and bottom harness. This saves the full dress but means double the work for the harness-cleaners. The bottom harness must be rifted out after the rehearsal and the top harness must be bliffed for the parade proper.

Within a couple of days the State Visit itself takes place. The Troop used only to fire a 41-Gun Salute 'to inform Her Majesty's subjects of Her guest's arrival to the Capital' but now we do a bit more. After the last round has been fired and echoes from the one-pound charge fade away, the Troop limbers up and leaves the front of the Saluting Base rather than galloping back up the Park. Then, in 'Column of Route' (one subsection behind the other), we stop on the Broadwalk and clean up before making our way through Apsley Gate and Wellington Arch down Constitution Hill to Buckingham Palace. The weather has a big influence on the format of this parade. If it is fine and the Park is dry the Troop will gallop into action in the normal way. If it is wet and boggy we are faced with a dilemma. Galloping ensures that the detachments, who are only inches behind the guns, are covered in mud literally from head to foot – which would not earn us too many marks as we stood outside Buckingham Palace to pay our compliments to Her Majesty and the visiting Head of State. Anything less than a gallop, spotted by a veteran Horse Gunner (circa The Great War or seemingly sometimes earlier) can start an avalanche of comment in the regimental magazine about the lack of dash, panache, etc, being shown by the custodians of RHA tradition, etc, etc; it is a fine balance and one takes one's choice. If it is decided to hold the State Visit at Windsor, even the 25-mile hack down there

'B' Sub in the Small Drive at Guildford. Note how close the markers are to the action. In muddy conditions they must keep their wits about them and be prepared to remove either their lances or themselves in double quick time from the path of a swinging gun.

(Above) Aldershot. Four breastcollars and two collar pads will take an hour or two to clean and polish.

(Below) Aldershot. 'Dismount'. Back in the lines (generally a tented village on the show-ground) the Troop dismounts from the still panting horses. The signal to actually drop out of the stirrup is given by the Lead Driver of the right-hand gun team.

will take less time than answering the letters and 'phone calls which follow a trotting salute in Hyde Park!

A couple of days later it is time for another rehearsal, this time The Queen's Birthday Parade or 'Trooping the Colour' as it is commonly known. This is, of course, primarily a Foot Guards parade, with the Troop providing the 'off stage' sound effects in the form of a Salute in Hyde Park. However, in 1973 a new tradition was introduced after a great deal of diplomatic correspondence initiated by the then CO, Major Tim Eastwood. The Troop now follows much the same drill as for State Visits, but actually ranks past Her Majesty outside Buckingham Palace once the battalion whose colours have been trooped has left the parade. If it were not specifically a Foot Guards parade the Troop, with guns on parade, would claim the privilege of ranking past the Queen first ... hence the diplomacy.

To ensure that the inmates of St John's Wood barracks don't relax too much at this time of year, in between the Trooping rehearsal and the parade proper we fire a Salute on the anniversary of the Duke of Edinburgh's birthday.

Between the Queen's Birthday Parade in June and the Royal Tournament in July there is time to fit the Drive in at a couple more shows. There are some hardy bi-annuals such as the Aldershot Army Display, whose wonderful old Rushmoor Arena has provided such a worthy setting for so many Drives over the decades: and premier agricultural shows such as the Three Counties, East of England, Great Yorkshire, and even the Royal itself. These shows are always very popular with the soldiers, as they are not purely military events and there is lots to do

Returning to the lines after a performance at Surrey County Show. There was a great deal of mud about after two days of continuous rain, and the detachment, riding close to the gun wheels (which have no mudguards) were spattered from head to foot.

and see over and above the hard work necessary to produce the Drive. It is for these civilian shows that the introduction of sponsors became a necessity. It is so expensive to move the Troop and house it under canvas that most shows are unable to meet the costs. In recent years the Troop has been most fortunate to have Dewhurst, the Master Butcher, as its chief sponsor, enabling it to perform at many shows all over the country.

The greater part of July is taken up with the Royal Tournament, at which the King's Troop has performed Musical Drives every year since 1948 without missing a performance. The Drive was associated with this, the ultimate in family shows, for many years before that. The inclusion of artillery at 'The Grand Military Tournament and Assault-at-Arms' in the Agricultural Hall, Islington, in the 1880s became a forerunner to the first Musical Drive by a Horse Artillery Battery from St John's Wood in 1891. The former was what we now call 'Gate Galloping' – ie teams negotiating a course, not dissimilar to that on the third day of a Three-Day Driving Event, as fast as possible; the latter was the Drive more or less as we know it today. All ranks also took part, as they still do, in the Skill at Arms competitions which figured so prominently in those early Tournaments. Tent-pegging, 'Cleaving the Turk's Head', and Sword, Lance and Revolver are still an historic and therefore very important part of the Tournament's heritage. Lastly, the show jumping competitions, which are the oldest in the country, form an

(Right) The inevitable rifting. After each performance, whether there be one or two a day, the harness has to be rifted and prepared for the next Display. The mild steel is very susceptible to rust, and must regularly be rifted to keep it gleaming.

Finishing touches are applied to Wendover's headcollar before the CO's inspection, Guildford.

A really good shine will last for a long time. Even after a performance in muddy conditions, once the sponge has been applied the really good 'bliff' will remain.

integral part of each Tournament, competed for with almost fanatical fervour by all ranks.

Despite the successful efforts of the Tournament's organisers to vary the programme from year to year, it doesn't change much for the Troop. Two sections hack down to Earl's Court on the Sunday before the show begins, while the other makes its way to Wellington Barracks in Birdcage Walk, where all the Tournament participants assemble for the publicity parade, known as the 'Mall March'. Recently this has grown in size, and provides a splendid spectacle for the thousands who turn out to watch all three Services march past to the sound of many bands.

By Sunday night the horses, about 60 in all, have been bedded down in stalls at the rear of the massive Exhibition Hall, while the soldiers are billeted on the first floor. I have only 'done' seven Tournaments but each year as I enter the dusty and noisy stable area, memories come flooding back of previous occasions when the Troop has occupied that same little corner of the nether regions. The Equitation Instructor is about to do his 21st consecutive show and always recalls horrendous stories of guns over, horses in the front row of the stalls, etc, etc . . . Suffice it to say that it has an atmosphere of its own and definitely holds a special place in our calendar.

In 16 days of performance we do 31 Drives – two a day except on Mondays when there is now only an evening performance; Sunday is a rest day. The arena measures 296 ft by 102 ft (90 m by 31 m) which, although marginally bigger than the old arena at Olympia where the Drive used to be performed, is still quite small when you consider that each gun team is 60 feet long. Margins for error are therefore minimal, and from time to time collisions do occur – though as a general rule they are of a minor nature, and no great harm befalls men, horses or equipment. The Earl's Court Drive demands considerable precision and each performance differs from the next. Success breeds speed, which in turn breeds greater risks, resulting in a stoppage of sorts which slows everyone down for a while until it speeds up again. Every now and again, inexplicably, nothing seems to go right. 1983 was one such year: in the first eight Drives we had seven stoppages, for a variety of reasons. Everyone's nerves were at breaking point, as a major disaster seemed inevitable. We even came in on Monday morning to practise, which was unheard of – yet still it went wrong. In desperation I rang up an ex-CO and asked him what to do. 'Sit and suffer like I had to', he replied. At least it had happened before! When we performed on the Monday night the pace was hand-canter only (I even saw a wheeler trotting), but the Drive was trouble-free. The following day was the same, and by Wednesday everything was back to normal. From then on we didn't have one more stoppage right through to the end of the Tournament – ie 22 Drives without a hitch. Such is the Royal Tournament and its own particular annual problems.

Tradition has it that after the final performance the Senior Section Commander (who might well have just driven in the last Drive) takes the Troop back to The Wood. On arrival he dismounts the Troop, files them away to water, and marches off himself. From that moment, as he leaves the square, his understudy, who had been 'flapping' anxiously ever since he finished his long Equitation Course in April, is the boss. He becomes Section Commander there and then: with a mixture of some 70 or 80 human and equine souls to look after until he, in turn, three years later to the night, hands them over to his replacement. It is a moment for both of them to remember.

In addition to the various domestic shows at which we perform the Musical Drive, we also go abroad if the calendar

Marquees provide plenty of room in which horses can live and men can work quite comfortably. Note that each horse is shackled to a heel-line, as there are no partitions. Shackles are swapped regularly to prevent sores and rope-burns.

permits. Overseas trips tend to fall into two categories. They are either Ministry of Defence-sponsored 'official' tours, which generally take place during the Show Season at the expense of a UK show; or 'private enterprise' ventures, organised by the Troop itself, the cost of which is borne by the show concerned. Both kinds of tour have much the same format, though the latter tends to take place in the late autumn or winter (in addition to our official programme) and are generally indoor shows. Because of the vast sums of money involved, as few as four or even two-gun displays are performed.

Needless to say, visits of either category are immensely popular with all ranks, although they mean a great deal of hard work and an immense amount of detailed planning by the Troop Captain and his staff. The logistical problems of moving 150 men, 80 horses, nine tons of guns and limbers, and an equal weight of freight – either by sea or air – are considerable. The paperwork alone for exporting such large numbers of horses is fairly daunting, but the Troop Veterinary Officers somehow manage to overcome the problems. It is amazing what one can get away with at border control points if uniform is worn. Government vets seem to lose their urge to check each horse's identity when 80 'look-alikes' are produced!

The Troop's foreign trips were initiated in the '60s. There was a trip by air to Denmark in '64, to Italy in '65, and then two years later to Expo '67 in Montreal, Canada. The Canadian trip was so popular that we have been trying to return there ever since. The latest estimate of cost for moving 54 men and 28 horses (plus two guns and freight) to Canada, accommodating them and getting them back to England is a quarter of a million dollars. It is not easy to secure this kind of sponsorship – especially when, as soldiers, we are restricted in what we may do in return. One company suggested that we should wear rosettes on our busbies advertising their product!

In an effort to reduce costs, a 'Mini Drive' with a reduced number of guns (for indoor shows only) has been devised. It is

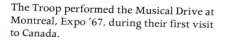

The Troop performed the Musical Drive at Montreal, Expo '67, during their first visit to Canada.

Firing the guns in the Olympic Stadium, Berlin, 1971, on the first of the Troop's three visits to the Berlin Tattoo.

amazing how, by astute use of lighting and music, a spectacular performance can be achieved with fewer guns, men and horses. The Two-Gun Drive was first produced at the Olympia Christmas Show in 1980. Because of an epidemic in their stables, the mounted police were unable to perform as originally planned, so the Troop received an urgent plea from the Show organisers just a week before 'curtain up'. Soldiers returned from leave, designed a display, practised it three times, and performed every night – hacking to and fro each day. A similar performance was extremely well received in Atlantic City, New Jersey, in 1982.

The Troop also performs at the Berlin Tattoo every six or seven years. This is an official engagement, and the full 'Earl's Court Drive' is mounted at the Deutschlandhalle, near the centre of the city. When we first went there in 1971, the horses were flown out in six loads of 15 horses on each flight. The Veterinary Officer broke the record for the number of visits to Berlin by one person in a day! Nowadays the horses travel by sea, which actually is more convenient, as we can take more spares. As well as Berlin, the Troop has performed in Holland, Paris and Ostend and has also sent detachments to enhance regimental parades in Germany.

CHAPTER SEVEN

Home and Away:
August to December

Until the early 1970s, when British Rail stopped transporting horses, the Troop moved by train.

THE SHOW SEASON officially ends with a Royal Salute to celebrate Her Majesty The Queen Mother's birthday on 4 August just a few days after the last performance at the Royal Tournament. But before individual training begins there are two important items on the calendar still to be fitted in: The Queen's Life Guard and Camp.

Each year since 1973 the Troop has relieved The Household Cavalry Regiment of their daily duty, mounting The Queen's Life Guard on Horse Guards parade in Whitehall, thus enabling them to go to their annual camp. Her Majesty is normally out of London during our three-week Guard period, so we have only to provide a Short Guard consisting of 12 men (plus four backroom boys) and 12 horses. Each guard is out of barracks for 24 hours, the handover to the New Guard being at 1100 daily.

While it is the Household Cavalry's bread and butter, it is quite a challenge for the King's Troop, and a most welcome annual event, although it involves a considerable amount of effort at the end of a busy show season. The black horses from Knightsbridge are rarely asked to move out of a walk or trot while on parade, so they are not required to be particularly fit to carry out the duties that they do so well. Our little chaps are in a totally different position. They are required to be galloping fit from the early spring right through to The Queen Mother's Salute and are naturally jumping out of their skins at this time of year. In exactly six days they have to forget about the scissors, the charge, and the 'gallop out', and must learn to walk, trot, and more importantly, stand still for two hours at a time.

As soon as the Salute has been accomplished, their feed is cut down, and training begins. Uniforms, which might be the worse for wear after the summer's activities, have to be changed and matched. NCOs must learn their orders, and the soldiers must practise the drills perfected by the Household Cavalry. Needless to say, we are well aware that the Troop's arrival on the scene will provoke increased interest from the officers of

The Blacks at the funeral of Field-Marshal
Earl Alexander of Tunis, 1969.

Headquarters London District which overlook Horse Guards,
and nothing can be left to chance. In short, we must aim to be
even better than those from whom we take over.

Horse Artillery uniform, both human and equine, does not
suit slow-moving or static parades. Since the RHA is well
known for its dash and panache, our kit is relatively straight-
forward, with no unnecessary embellishments which would
prevent a man from mounting or dismounting at trot or canter
or serving the guns. It thus has to be absolutely spotless in all
respects to withstand close inspection at the halt; it does not
boast the sheepskin, chains, 'whites' or gleaming cuirasses of
the heavy cavalry. Consequently, The Queen's Life Guard
imposes a different kind of discipline on all ranks and on our
horses, as well as ensuring that our kit is 100 per cent up to the
mark at the end of the season. All in all, therefore, it is a very
good exercise for the Troop....

When we have handed back the duties of The Queen's Life
Guard to its rightful custodians, the Troop once again completely
changes its life style, and each section goes off to Camp.
Although a certain amount of military training takes place,
especially Fitness Training, it is more of an Adventure Training

81

Firing a Salute in Hyde Park

1. (Left) File Out. The horses are led out on to the square to be 'hooked in' to the guns which are pushed out from the gun park by the limber gunners. The Number One supervises this operation and ensures that everything is in order before the Section Commanders come out of the Mess to inspect both their subsections.

2. (Above) The CO's Inspection. When the Troop is formed up, with the officers on parade, the CO (whether he is riding on parade or not) carries out his inspection before they move off.

3. (Below) Moving Off. As the Troop marches out of barracks an 'Eyes Left' is given to the CO standing on the steps of the Mess.

4. (Left) Marble Arch. The Troop traditionally passes through Marble Arch at the north end of the Park before and after firing the Salute.

5. (Below) Galloping into Action. The six teams gallop at full stretch past the Saluting Base.

6. (Right) The Salute. Forty-one rounds are fired every ten seconds, usually at noon. Each round comprises a one-pound charge which in the right atmospheric conditions can be heard for many miles. The teams, having dropped off the guns, gallop back to the Marble Arch end of the Park to await the completion of the Salute.

Her Majesty The Queen's visit to the Royal Regiment of Artillery in Dortmund, 1984. The Troop provided the escort – the Commanding Officer on Dr Sebastian and four soldiers riding black horses from 'F' Sub.

The Troop GS wagon is used to resupply the stables at Horse Guards Parade during Queen's Life Guard.

exercise than a military one. After the rigours of the previous four or five months, each section is encouraged to organise its own programme of events during the 10 days or so that it is out of barracks.

I personally prefer section camps rather than a Troop camp. They allow each Section Commander to choose his own site and have autonomous command of his section for a change. For financial reasons each location must be within 100 miles of St John's Wood, and most sections end up on the coast, occupying farm buildings or the stables of a large country house. From their camp sites they sally forth for a multitude of activities, the most popular of which is swimming the horses. Most horses, given the correct introduction, will thoroughly enjoy a swim in the sea, which is very good for them. Troop horses love it, and so do the soldiers. Whatever the weather, in they go at all hours of the day before racing up and down the beaches, or having tug o' war matches in the shallows. These activities always attract a large audience of holiday-makers and locals alike, who usually take a great interest in the sections' camp activities.

At the end of Camp it is usual for a section to organise a show of some description in aid of a local charity. In between the swimming, mounted orienteering, boat trips and general adventure training, practice for the show continues until finally quite a high standard of performance is reached. When I make my visits I am always amazed how close the section and the local community have become in so short a time. On my first visit, I could not believe it when Left Section took on the local village tug o'war team (mounted on our horses) and got beaten in two straight pulls – proving that a 17-stone advantage is worth more than horsemanship!

When the camps are over it is time once more to change the tempo of life at The Wood. Towards the end of October there is generally a State Visit which requires a 41-Gun Salute in Hyde Park and a rank past Buckingham Palace. This in turn means a couple of trips down to Wormwood Scrubs to practice. It will have been 10 to 11 weeks since a Salute has been fired and, as usual, nothing must be left to chance.

Mid-October sees the beginning of what is termed 'individual training', which applies both to men and horses. Soldiers have to upgrade as Mounted Gunners, to increase both their usefulness to the Troop and their pay. To this end a number of courses are run under the direction of the Troop Captain. These include lectures on veterinary matters, horsemastership, equitation and a host of other military/equine subjects, as

'C' Sub's rodeo team during the Drivers' Ride finale.

Remembrance Sunday. The 'Minute Guns' return from Horse Guards via Hyde Park Corner and give an 'Eyes Left' to the Royal Artillery War Memorial.

well as a variety of practical work. At the end of the eight-week training period (interrupted by the Lord Mayor's Show and Remembrance Sunday), each soldier to be upgraded takes an examination, both written and oral.

At the same time four rides take place – Recruits, Recruits 'Follow Up', Detachment, and Drivers. Instructors from within the Troop are nominated to set the programme and to conduct the instruction from start to finish. Each ride culminates in a 'Pass Out' ride, when the CO decides which men have successfully completed their riding course. This is a very important day for the soldiers, as a thumbs down on the Pass Out means that they cannot progress within the Troop, which also affects their pay and prospects.

For a recruit it is doubly important. Until he is passed out by the CO he is not allowed to ride exercise in the morning, the first sign that a young soldier is losing his recruit or 'chunky' status. The standard to be achieved is necessarily quite high, as it is not easy to ride one and lead two corn-fed horses through the streets of London.

The Recruits 'Follow Up' is exactly what it sounds like – a ride designed for those soldiers who are not yet able to ride on parade in detachment but who have progressed beyond a basic recruit's standard.

The Detachment Ride is designed for soldiers who will be riding on parade the following season. Instructors concentrate on sword drill, mounting and dismounting from both sides at

trot and canter, and riding school drill work. The RSM concentrates on gun drill. In addition to parade skills, some jumping instruction is also given, and a competition is held at the end of the Ride. Competition instruction is not limited to ride periods, and any soldier who has proved himself competent enough to his Number One is encouraged to ride in his spare time and to practise for the many show-jumping competitions and events for which the Troop enters *en bloc*.

The old Weedon jumping lessons down the grid still hold good for the modern mounted soldier, and all the soldiers 'fly' down the jumping lanes with arms folded, taking their jackets off or shouting out their name, rank, and number. If a soldier concentrates on achieving these aims, between jumping the first and leaving the end of the grid, he is quite likely to end up in the correct jumping position.

The Drivers' Ride naturally enough concentrates – as much as possible – on team work. It is not easy to strike the correct balance between proficiency in driving skills and over-using the horses, so we aim to carry out two full draught parades per week. To start with, the drivers practise with teams of six horses, not connected and without a gun. Whip drill is taught in this manner as are the patterns of the drive and the theory of driving. Seasoned drivers take part in the ride, so the novices quickly learn by their good example. Once the patterns have been established, the teams are 'hooked in' and the Scrubs becomes their schooling ground. Competitions such as 'gate galloping' are used to encourage the dash and accuracy required for a good drive. The 'Pass Out' actually incorporates a full drive at the canter, which lays the foundations for a smooth start to Troop training the following spring.

The March Past at the Royal Tournament. All the drivers, except the Lead Driver of the nearest team, cut their head and eyes away to the left and put their whips over.

In 1984, encouraged by Colonel Sir Mike Ansell and his book *Soldier On*, the Drivers' Ride also included a trick-riding competition. Each sub had to devise a ride lasting five minutes, and many new skills not seen in the old Riding School for several years emerged. They provided great entertainment for all ranks, and a lot of hard work went in to producing a variety of performances. I especially liked the 'Cowboy and Indian' act from C Sub where, among other imaginative exploits, a remount, complete with imitation horns, was roped, 'thrown' to the ground and branded; a few marks were lost because the 'steer' refused to get up when it was all over! A dressage/driving quadrille from B Sub, copied from the Warendorf stallions, also gained high marks, while D Sub's balancing act defied gravity and description. The winners, B Sub, were presented with an engraved cartridge case, to be held until next season's exploits take place.

Inevitably the drivers are the best riders in the Troop, and a fair amount of competition work also takes place. Show jumping in the school, cross-country schooling at Tweseldown, and drag hunting, all form part of the syllabus.

The only other ride that takes place during individual training is the Officers' Ride. During my time as CO I have taken this myself, usually in the early mornings. It takes the form of a jumping lesson or a kit ride, when the officers, complete with busbies and swords, go through the drill required on parade. At the end of each ride the Adjutant conducts

Inter-subsection tug o' war is a favourite pastime for both men and horses.

'D' Sub's balancing act, part of their contribution to the Drivers' Ride.

a 10-minute session of sword drill before the chargers are returned to their stables for breakfast.

The working year ends in early December with the Pass-Out Rides, the course exams, and the review of remounts. Unless we have been lucky enough to arrange an indoor show abroad, half the Troop goes on leave at this time, leaving the remainder to keep the barracks 'ticking over' during the Christmas holiday period. 'Ticking over' includes putting the newly-broken remounts into draught for the first time, the Junior NCOs Cadre Course, and Army Saddle Clubs Association course, and 'winter training' at Melton Mowbray.

89

Her Majesty The Queen's Birthday Parade.
'C' and 'D' Subs rank past Buckingham
Palace after Her Majesty has returned from
Horse Guards Parade with the Battalion
whose colours have been trooped.

CHAPTER EIGHT

The Horses

O F THE 120 OR SO HORSES that the Troop has on its books, 13 are chargers and the remainder are lines horses, officially designated in army terms as 'Ride and Drive'. We are actually established for 111 horses in all, but usually have a dozen or so extra as the remounts learn their trade and the oldies hang on 'just in case' ...

They are nearly all bought in the Irish Republic, as they have been for generations, from two main dealers. These two men, experienced in the Army's needs, scour Ireland for the right animals, having received a shopping list from the mounted units via the Royal Army Veterinary Corps who are ultimately responsible for their purchase. The three main users are the RAVC Depôt at Melton which needs a variety of animals for instructional purposes, the Household Cavalry Regiment, and the Troop itself. While the Household Cavalry need only black horses of substance for both officers and troopers, or greys for the trumpeters, we require a rather more varied selection.

Not only do we need different colours – light bay, dark bay, brown and black, but we also require a variety of sizes to maintain the correct line of draught. Leaders should be 16 hands, centres 15.3, and wheelers 15.2 or even smaller if they are of stocky build. As soldiers have got bigger over the years ('too much free milk and honey, Sir,' says RSM Clark) so the sizes have gradually increased; we now have some leaders as big as 16 hands. Officially described as 'Light Irish Draught', they are in fact a light type of cob. The kind of horse described in an earlier chapter, which was sought for those early RHA Troops, still holds good today: short-legged, open-chested, broad-winded, etc.

I personally have been buying and selling horses most of my life but was still fascinated when I went with two veterinary officers on the annual Buying Commission to Ireland. One by one the horses were produced for inspection by small boys in large caps. They were looked at, 'listened to' and then trotted up, lunged or ridden, depending on their state of education. The majority were (meant to be) unbroken. All the customary haggling and 'formalities' were gone through – a ritual that has

All army horses have their numbers stamped on their feet. In the days when they were killed in battle the foot had to be returned to prove that the horse had not been sold or lost.

(Right) A Wheeler dressed for action: hip-long wheel (cross straps); breeching (part of the braking system); traces, wire-adjustable. (Below) The pole-bar supporting-strap is attached to the pole-bar (which is made of teak). The draught pole is slipped through the pole-bar at one end and attached to the limber at the other.

been performed for decades. I knew more or less what I was in for when I arrived at the yard of one famous dealer. 'I don't think you've met Major Wallace,' said the Colonel ... 'Ah sure and I must be the only man in Ireland who hasn't' came the warm reply. We bought about 30 horses from him, making a total of 46, of which 16 were destined for the Troop. Then a deal had to be struck with the shipper who was responsible for getting them safely to Melton the following week. After more haggling and a glass or two of whisky, a fair deal was arrived at which was within our allowed budget, and both sides were well satisfied with the day's business.

When the horses arrive at Melton they are given a very thorough veterinary examination, with any failures being returned. They then have their feet dressed and go into isolation for observation before being turned out to grass for the summer. It is a vital period for us, as during this time they are regularly handled and shod by the skilled staff at the Depôt, making our job so much easier when it comes to breaking them. In the five or six months during which the remounts await issue, any shortfall in the 'Irish Buy' is made up by local purchase in England and Wales. Unremarkably, the rituals are identical, though on a smaller scale.

The remounts are finally collected and boxed down to Larkhill in October where they spend seven or eight weeks in the hands of the Troop remount riders. The Troop doesn't have a special cadre of men to do this job, but sends down a team of 10 riders under the Equitation Instructor and a Section Commander to back these youngsters and prepare them for draught work, which is the next stage of their training. What a rewarding job it is, too – a blissful couple of months away from London, encouraging uneducated, ignorant 'hairies' to take their first steps toward a life of ceremonial duties. It is very popular with all ranks, who just for this short time can relax a bit away from the eagle eye of the RSM and literally let their hair down. It must amaze the personnel of the Royal School of Artillery as they go about their business of practising for modern warfare with all its sophisticated electronic gadgetry, to see a dozen or so remounts being long-reined through the Guided Weapons Wing en route for the manège.

At the end of this happy stint the Section Commanders and Numbers One go down to the Plain and watch the end-product being put through their paces. The shaggy monsters of October, having been clipped and trimmed, perform immaculately in the Riding School over a course of coloured poles, and then jump a small cross-country course. Most of us return to The Wood well satisfied with the job that has been done. Draught training begins when they arrive back in barracks.

I have the most wonderful memories of these versatile little horses who have given all ranks at The Wood so much enjoyment. What they lack in class they make up for in guts and temperament. Basically they pull guns for a living, but in addition they are used for instructional rides, show jumping, eventing, the Troop point-to-point, hunting, trick-riding, and a variety of games, such as tug o'war, which they greatly enjoy.

Troop horses tend to develop into 'characters' as they get on

During morning exercise the Troop rides 'one to three', differing from the Household Cavalry, who ride 'one to two'.

94

Two of 'A' Sub's light bay Wheelers, who represent all that is best in RHA draught horses.

in life, and some have some rather unconventional habits. When I commanded Right Section in the early '70s I had two such characters in B Sub – Joey (whose real name was Oakleigh, named after Major O'Grady. All Troop horses' names begin with the first letter of the current CO's surname) who was 21, and Albert (Hereford, after Heaton-Ellis) who was a young lad of 17. These two had lived together with only a 'swinging bale' separating them for years. Joey was in the team and Albert was ridden by the CO's trumpeter. One day, Tim Eastwood, my CO at the time, said that Joey was too old for the team and Albert was too ugly to be his trumpeter's horse, so the two should swap places. From then on they had to be separated. From sharing each other's mangers – which they had done for as long as anyone could remember – they constantly tried to kick and bite each other, with the result that they had to be put at opposite ends of the lines.

Troop horses are a very philosophical bunch, as I experienced at the Tidworth Three-Day Event in 1973. I was riding a leader from A Sub called Barbican (No 54 and 'Sparky' to his friends)

95

Tent-pegging at the Royal Windsor Show.

who was 12 years old and had spent all his life in the team. Ventures of this kind were totally new to him, but he was the sort who'd try anything – at least once. I had spent considerable time teaching him to jump into water – which at first, not unreasonably, he was disinclined to do. However, after much 'encouragement' he got the hang of it and was only too eager to oblige. When we arrived at the Bourne Crossing – an obstacle of some width – 'Sparky' jumped straight in. We both disappeared for a short while, and when we emerged he had obviously taken quite a lot of water on board, as he coughed and panted for breath, with water pouring out of his ears. Eventually, reckoning he had recovered, we pressed on. Sparky however had in fact had enough of Three-Day Eventing, and when he got to the Hay Rack he jumped in it, refused to budge, and started eating the hay. I had to dismount in a state of utter embarrassment while no lesser persons than Lord Hugh Russell and Richard Meade removed the rack from around him; Sparky had made his point.

I remember on another occasion when out hunting with the Quorn on a B Sub Leader called Ronald we were matching strides with Chris Collins on none other than the great Credit Call. Chris, who much admired 'Snaky Neck', as he called him, remarked after a chase of some few miles, how amazing it was that an animal costing £630 who pulled a gun for his living could happily bowl along beside the best hunter 'chaser in the country. They are truly remarkable little horses, and it is a great relief to know that they'll never be asked to suffer the depredations of war like their predecessors.

The officers' horses are known as 'chargers' and are of a different type to the 'hairies', but still bought in Ireland by the Buying Commission. It is important that they be substantial to look at and stand no less than 16.3. An officer weighing 13 stone or more, wearing Full Dress and sitting on a regimental saddle complete with sheepskin and shabraque needs a large conveyance if he isn't going to appear under-horsed. Temperament is also most important, in order to achieve steadiness on parade. A lines horse in detachment can get away with a small amount of fidgeting whereas an officer's horse out in front must be rock-steady. They may be any colour, but at least one black is required as the 'funeral charger'.

I have rather discouraged officers from over-using their chargers for sport in addition to their parade work, as I felt that these half- or three-quarter-bred horses were being expected to do too much. Army prices do not allow for much quality

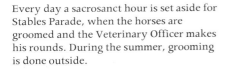

Every day a sacrosanct hour is set aside for Stables Parade, when the horses are groomed and the Veterinary Officer makes his rounds. During the summer, grooming is done outside.

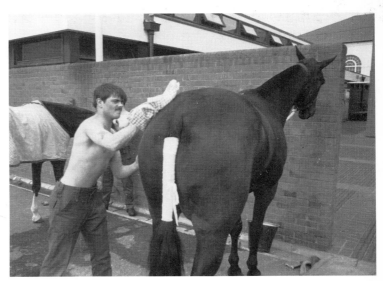

While at Larkhill this remount showed a particular penchant for lying down, so later she featured prominently in the Trick Ride. Unfortunately she disgraced herself by refusing to get up!

within the confines of the mandatory requirements that I have mentioned, and chargers were being asked to do things beyond their capabilities; this sometimes meant that unprepared horses were being used on parade too early. The alternative is for officers to buy or borrow 'private' horses (capable of going on parade) or to ride Troop horses who, despite their lack of height, are generally better able to carry out a variety of roles without fear or favour.

In the days gone by, when army money could purchase a higher class of animal, a great many chargers won substantial prizes, both at home and abroad. In the early days of Badminton Horse Trials, for example, every officer was expected to ride his charger there – and did. Of late, this sadly has not been the case. Now and again a 'freak' horse appears in the lines, and provides his rider with a chance to have a go at competitions normally beyond our reach. One such horse is a 16.3 black charger called Dr Sebastian (named, like all the chargers, after a Surtees character) who was issued to me as an unbroken three-year-old in 1971.

From an early age Sebastian impressed me with his willingness and ability to please. Despite his round and common action he was always among the ribbons in dressage competitions, ran second in his only point-to-point, and won his first official BHS Horse Trial, having never been across country before. In addition to his extra-mural activities he took to parade work like a veteran and, even as a four-year-old, was a pleasure to sit on. His three and a half years with me reached its zenith with a clear round at Badminton as a seven-year-old and resulted in our being short-listed for a place in the Three-Day Event World Championships. Although we didn't make it, our association

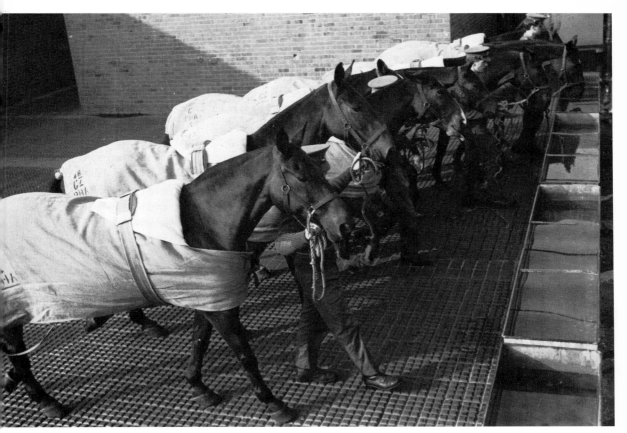

'File to water from the left.' Twice a day all the horses are led out to water, although there is an automatic watering system in the stables. It gives them a breath of fresh air and enables Section Commanders to compare the teams for colour match, tail lengths, etc.

did not stop there. He sadly got a bit of heat in his leg, so I took him to see Peter Scott-Dunn, the British team vet, and sought his valuable advice. 'Rest him during the winter, restrict him to parade work only, and if you are ever lucky enough to command one day, he should be waiting for you ...!' I have ridden him on every parade since I returned to The Wood eight years later.

By and large the horses stay in the Troop longer than the soldiers, each giving an average of ten years' service. Thus when officers and men return to The Wood for a visit they head straight for the lines to meet their old friends. There's a fair chance that after a period of six or seven years away one could walk through the barracks and not recognise any two-legged inmates at all – many of one's old comrades having moved on to 'better' things. It is most reassuring, therefore, to visit the horses who, although not able to move on, seem content with the life that they are living. Without doubt it is they who are the soul of the Troop, responsible for its atmosphere and unity.

99

CHAPTER NINE

The Men

'Boots and Saddles' – twenty minutes before 'File Out'. A Wheel Driver carries out his wheel set.

BEFORE ANY SOLDIER joins the Troop, from either the Junior Leaders Regiment at Bramcote or the Depôt Regiment at Woolwich, he comes to The Wood first as a civilian for a week's attachment. The object of this unique exercise is two-fold: firstly it allows us to have a good look at a man and to ascertain whether he is suitable to fill a much sought-after vacancy; and secondly it allows him to see at first hand what life in a busy mounted unit is really like. So often a lad is taken by the glamour of the Troop on parade and does not see beyond the bands playing, the dash of the Drive, and the thunderous applause which accompanies it. It is important that he should see for himself, and even participate in, the hard work that goes to produce the end-product. After a week with us (some do not last that long) he is interviewed by the Adjutant who is given a written report by the NCOs of the Sub with which he has been working.

This daunting exercise befell me in 1966 just before I went off to Mons Officer Cadet School. To step out of 'civvy street' as a young man and be thrown in at the deep end with no knowledge of the Troop or even the Army is indeed an amazing experience. Everything is new. I thought I knew how to groom, bed down, and ride when I entered the barrack gates of The 'old' Wood. Not so! Even two years as a student at Colonel Joe Dudgeon's famous Burton Hall Equestrian Centre in County Dublin had not prepared me for the 'Army way' of doing things. I was not spared, and nor are today's visitors. Reveille at 0600 hours, mucking out, grooming and polishing, plus all the normal daily duties, are part of the potential soldier's diet. I remember polishing swords and sweeping the square until I was exhausted, and then looking at my watch to see that it was only 8.30 am. It is a worthwhile experience and goes a long way to preventing wastage. We are always playing a tight numbers game when it comes to recruiting, and it is important not to waste a precious vacancy on a man who won't measure up to the standards demanded.

The majority of the soldiers in the Troop, unlike their mechanised counterparts are from the country and have prob-

Members of the Troop took part in the film 'Far From the Madding Crowd'.

ably ridden before enlisting. Those with Pony Club backgrounds are the best material, as they have been correctly taught the basics of horse management. I am inclined to be a bit nervous of ex-lads from racing, as they tend to bring their bad habits with them which can spread like wildfire. I remember seeing two 'refugees from Newmarket' going into the Riding School for their first Recruits Ride, taken by the Equitation Instructor, Sergeant-Major Eric Witts – himself an ex-jockey and now a successful trainer. These two poor souls, virtually straight off the Heath, trotted in with their knees under their chins and swinging their whips like (they thought) the great Lester Piggott in a tight finish ... The roar that greeted them could have been heard in Westminster, and an hour later a couple of very chastened potential champion jockeys had taken their first faltering steps, the 'Army way'.

101

The 'Staff Employed' Parade. At 0830 all those soldiers who do not work in the lines assemble to sweep the barracks – much to the enjoyment of the 'Linesmen'.

Most soldiers are, of course, keen to get on parade as soon as they possibly can and be part of the great spectacle. However, it takes a while to learn the various drills and skills required to ride in detachment and to form part of a gun team, so they start as 'markers'. This is probably the most dangerous job on parade as, with their lances, they mark out the arena of the Small Drive which takes place during the outside Display. When the ground is wet and the guns are sliding they have to keep their wits about them. A swinging gun can be very dangerous. On more than one occasion I have seen a marker drop his lance and run like a hare to avoid disaster. I shall never forget at Harrogate Show the sight of Gunner Luke marching (in rather wobbly fashion) out of the arena, coming smartly to attention in the collecting ring, and promptly keeling over unconscious, with his ankle broken in three places where a gun had hit him. Despite the risk of being hit – which does not happen very

102

often – most soldiers are delighted to get the chance, and they work hard to improve their drills so as not to let the Troop down.

From the job of marker a soldier can move on quite quickly, depending largely on his previous riding experience and his own personal ambition. The next logical step is to ride in Detachment, either as a Gun Number or Horse Holder; most men spend two or even three seasons in this employment. The final step on parade is to drive in the team itself. In days of yore, Drivers were a separate entity within a Battery. Now it is a job just like any other, but undoubtedly has the most kudos attached to it.

Soldiers, like remounts, start in the centre position to learn the basics of their trade – which primarily is to keep the traces taut so as to prevent a 'leg-over'. Having spent a season or two in this position, a Driver will then graduate to the Wheel, where he is ultimately responsible for the accurate steering of his gun. The Lead Driver points the team in the right direction but it is the Wheel Driver who is actually responsible for the finer points of steering. Lead Driver, the senior job among the junior ranks, is the ultimate in responsibility and skill.

Any soldier who attains this position of importance is probably in at least his fifth year at The Wood, has one or two tapes on his arm, and possesses a high degree of nerve, skill and dash. He is responsible for the placing of his team in the right position at the right time, and with him rests the unenviable task of split-second decisions, especially if an error is made by either his own team or – more likely – someone else's. Just as the Team Drivers must have the ultimate faith in their Lead

A Wheel Driver unfastens his surcingle while a 'back-room boy' waits for the inside traces to be undone.

Sergeant Ben Jones (left) in his early days
with the Troop.

Driver, so he in turn must completely trust the other Lead
Drivers, especially the Battery Leader or Senior Lead Driver
who sets the pace throughout the Drive.

By the time a man has reached this sort of responsible
position on parade he also has special duties within the lines.
He may be responsible to his Number One for overseeing the
equipment or the horses, and most certainly for the welfare of
the Gunners in his Sub. By this stage of his career any such man
might be sent on the much coveted Equitation Course at
Melton, where after six months he attains a certificate qualify-
ing him to instruct back in barracks.

As a senior man within his empire he will get first choice
(after the Number One) of the better horses if he feels inclined to
go show jumping or eventing. Prowess at these sports, coupled
with a responsible attitude, can point his career through Subsection Number One towards the post of Equitation Instructor.

104

This in turn entails a two-year tour at Melton, instructing on the various courses there and gaining valuable experience and expertise much needed at The Wood on his return to Troop duty.

The most celebrated Equitation Instructor of recent times was the Olympic Three-Day Event Gold Medallist, Ben Jones. Gunner (now Captain) Jones joined the Troop in 1952 and served at The Wood until 1968 before moving to Melton Mowbray as the Senior Instructor under Major Ron Hill. I was lucky enough to benefit from his instruction on my course and to see and appreciate at first hand his appetite for hard work, without which he would not have gained his many successes. During his time at the top of this most demanding of sports he rode his Troop horse Sherpa and a charger, Master Bernard, in a variety of British teams, including that at the Tokyo Olympics in 1964 (on Master Bernard). His greatest accolade was his team

Sergeant (now Captain) Ben Jones riding a Troop horse, Master Bernard, at Burghley Horse Trials in 1964

Early morning at the Scrubs. Steam rises from 'A' Sub's Leaders, Flossie and Tatler, after the first cantering drives. On most Draught Parade days three drives are practised: one at the trot, two at the canter.

gold medal in 1968 at the Mexico Olympics, on The Poacher. Now a civilian, Ben Jones continues to win prizes on the domestic scene and to spread the gospel, which he first learned at The Wood, to his civilian students.

Not everyone, of course, can attain the standards of excellence achieved by the few Ben Jones's of this world, and for lesser mortals on attaining the rank of Bombardier, or even Sergeant, a decision has to be made. Although a soldier may serve all of his 22 years with the Troop it is not always in his, or the Troop's, best interests. Until quite recently it was the exception rather than the rule that a man would leave The Wood and seek his fortune elsewhere. Nowadays, however, for those not necessarily tied to an equestrian career it is becoming more common for NCOs to join one of the many Royal Artillery regiments in order to widen their experience and so produce a better NCO. In time, these 'old boys' return to St John's Wood

NAAFI break at Wormwood Scrubs. A Driver shares his 'Scrubs Cake' after a morning's practice on the cinders.

one or two ranks higher, to fill the senior posts on the Troop's establishment and pass on the wealth of experience that they have gained during their time with a 'service' regiment.

As NCOs leave to join other regiments, so promotions are created annually for successors snapping at their heels. As a general rule they are cross-posted to another section on promotion. At the end of each show season, which is the time for posting and promotions, the Troop experiences quite a large change of key personnel, and during the late autumn and winter months they have time to settle in to their new jobs before the pressures of the Training and Show Season in the following spring and summer.

Needless to say, not every soldier can attain NCO rank or see himself as a Number One or higher. Sadly, therefore, a number of senior Gunners, usually at the six-year stage, leave the Troop to try their hand in 'civvy street' – most probably in the horse

world. It is, of course, a fact of life that people move on, but the Troop depends largely on the experience of these six- and nine-year men, and their departure is a great loss. It is sometimes possible to place such soldiers in the Troop trades already described, where not only do they guarantee themselves a living in later life but can also achieve 'time promotion' if they prove themselves capable of carrying higher rank.

Many of these ex-gunners return to The Wood year after year at our annual reunions and can regularly be seen at Earl's Court, Hyde Park or County Shows. Some, such as ex-National Service soldiers Paddy McMahon, Barry Hills, and Bill Rees, attain the highest ranks of their chosen profession. Few totally sever their links with the Troop, demonstrating the camaraderie engendered within the small acreage at The Wood.

The highlight of section camps is swimming the horses in the sea, and galloping them on the beach. The picture shows Right Section at Bembridge, Isle of Wight.

CHAPTER TEN

The Officers

SELECTION FOR HORSE ARTILLERY has been dealt with in an earlier chapter, so I will not dwell on it unduly. Suffice it to say that it is regarded as more important to post a good officer to The Wood than a good horseman. Sadly, as the years go by it becomes increasingly more difficult to find both qualities in one man. It is in fact now quite common for an officer to be posted to St John's Wood who has never sat on a horse in his life. What a challenge!

In the early days of this century, as equestrian sports began to figure more and more prominently in international competition, it was quite common to find Horse Gunners representing their country in a variety of them. With notable exceptions, it is probably fair to say that show jumping and eventing were better suited to the skills (and pocket) of RHA officers than polo and racing. Fortunately, however, all these sports were *de rigeur* to a greater or lesser extent right across the world wherever 'ball button' regiments or batteries were located.

The RHA was represented in the Three-Day Event, then known as the 'Military', at the 1924 Paris Olympics by Lieutenant (later Brigadier) Todd and Captain (later General) EB 'Dolly' de Fonblanque. In the 1936 Berlin Olympics no fewer than five Gunners competed. Captain (now Lieutenant-General) ED Howard-Vyse, who was ex Riding Troop and a Weedon instructor, won a bronze medal in the Three-Day Event; Captain 'Buggins' Brunker rode in the Show Jumping team; Captain 'Frizz' Fowler, of J Battery RHA, rode five of his own home-trained ponies to win a silver medal in the Polo; Lieutenant (now Major-General) John Sheffield of D Battery ran in the 440 yards Hurdles; and Lieutenant Rampling competed in the 440 yards Sprint and the 440 yards Relay, in which he won a gold medal.

In the London Olympic Games of 1948 Colonel Henry Nicoll, a keen Three-Day Event competitor, also demonstrated his show jumping prowess by winning a team bronze, on Kilgeddin. The course must have been quite tricky, as 21 of the 44 competitors were eliminated. (It is interesting to note that these were the first Games in which civilians were allowed to ride.)

A group of officers outside the Mess at the time of the Coronation in 1953. (Left to right) Lt Christopher Morgan, Capt Derrick Dyson, Major Frank Weldon, Capt Ian Castle, Lt David Vandeleur, Lt Brian Barber.

Brigadier Lindon Bolton RHA also rode in the Three-Day Event team.

At the Royal Tournament, the King's Cup and Prince of Wales Cup – the blue ribands of service jumping – were very nearly an RHA benefit from the early '20s to the late '30s.

As I have already mentioned, it is now more difficult to find an officer with such competitive skills. But the Royal Regiment is still comparatively large and has many officers from a wide cross-section of the community within its ranks. Every year one Subaltern must be found, not necessarily from an RHA regiment, to go on the Long Course at Melton. Two years out of three a Captain must also be posted in as Adjutant or Troop Captain. The Commanding Officer usually serves for two and a half years, and ideally should have served previously as a Section Commander.

On arrival at The Wood, whichever regiment an officer has come from, he is entering a very different world. I personally have served only in Field Artillery RHA, but I am sure that life in any regiment is much the same whatever discipline you

The Officers' Tent-Pegging Team at the
Royal Windsor Show, 1984.

happen to specialise in, be it Air Defence, Locating, or Heavy
Artillery. They have the same problems with sophisticated
equipment and vehicles, and share the same pressures on
exercises or impending moves.

A different set of problems awaits an officer at The Wood.
He must learn from scratch what the majority of his soldiers
take for granted – about lameness, illness, the problems of
remounts, draught work, ceremonial duties which previously
he has only seen on TV, and a host of other peculiarities. A little
knowledge is a dangerous thing, and it is best to enter this
strange world with an open mind.

The Long Course at Melton gives one a very necessary
six–month 'breaking-in' period where the difficulties of lasers
and radar rapidly fade into the background as backing your

112

remount for the first time becomes the number one problem. Throughout the duration of the Course the officers from The Wood turn up at weekends, to squeeze in a day's hunting before Remembrance Sunday, the State Opening or, worse still, the snow. It is a good opportunity for the incoming officers to pick brains and to get a feel for what is happening in London. On this demanding course those with a Pony Club or a hunting/racing background undoubtedly have the edge over the others, but it is tremendous fun whichever way you look at it.

On arrival at The Wood in April the new world awaits. On joining, all officers, whether they be Section Commander, Adjutant or Captain, go into the lines for a period of grooming, riding exercise – including 'Roughex' (with only a blanket as saddle) – and all the other duties of a mounted Gunner. There are also a number of courses to attend, which increase one's usefulness during a tour of duty – firefighting, catering, NBC

Outside the Officers' Mess, the Adjutant is about to drive off in the Troop dog cart with a 'D' Sub pair, Wharfdale and Turnstile.

Section Commander's Horse Inspection, which takes place before the CO's Inspection. The Veterinary Officer is always on hand.

(Nuclear, Biological and Chemical warfare), or worst of all – Accounts. Section Commanders have to use these months wisely, as not only must they attend at least two of the courses but they will also be responsible for the barracks and its contents while the Troop is at shows, and they must learn all about their job and memorise the names and numbers of all their 'look-alike' horses, not to mention their men.

A tour with the Troop provides a wonderful opportunity for officers to ride in a variety of ways. Some specialise in a certain discipline and try to perfect it, while others become a 'jack of all trades'. During my own tour as Section Commander I took up eventing and pursued it – within the confines of my job – fairly seriously. I had never evented before, other than in the Pony Club, but the Troop allowed me during my three-year tour to make progress, though with only moderate success; during my tour in Command I have concentrated on racing.

The Equitation Instructor, CO, and Senior Section Commander (right) watching a Drive practice, down at the Scrubs.

The Veterinary Officer anaesthetizes a nasty tread before stitching it up.

My successor, while a Section Commander, did everything including an International Driving Three-Day Event in the Troop Wagon. We have had the dog-cart overhauled and it awaits his arrival!

The one common denominator among the officers is hunting, which stands us all in good stead for whatever equestrian pursuit we choose. As already mentioned, it gives one a far higher degree of confidence than any amount of riding school drilling, and confidence on parade is of the utmost importance for officers with little previous riding experience.

The influence of RHA officers on equestrian sport particularly applies to horse trials, and the Troop has produced some notables, both as riders and as administrators. In each of these categories Lieutenant-Colonel Frank Weldon, who commanded from 1949 to 1954, must surely take pride of place. Not only did he achieve the highest Olympic and international honours but he has continued to influence the sport as an international judge and adviser, in addition to his vital role as Director of the world's premier Three-Day Event at Badminton.

Colonel Frank's successes as a rider on his famous horse Kilbarry are clearly linked to the Troop, and to the barracks at St John's Wood. The great horse was not, as is popularly thought, a charger, but was bought from a farmer called Roland Farrow near Newark. As CO, Major Weldon visited Mr Farrow as a potential National Service Recruit and ended up buying Kilbarry with a view to winning the Gunner Gold Cup at Sandown. This he subsequently achieved in 1955 and 1956 on a horse called Snowshill Jim, which was bought as an eventer to replace Kilbarry!

Major (later Lieut.-Col.) Frank Weldon on his great Three-Day Event horse Kilbarry.

Kilbarry, secured for £750 as a five-year old, did in fact win a race at Larkhill in 1951 before going in the wind as a result of a 'flu epidemic which swept through The Wood that winter. He was Hobdayed in the Riding School by 'Mouse' Townsend, but although this helped a lot it was not completely successful, and effectively put a stop to what might have been a fruitful racing career. Eventing was the natural second choice, and Kilbarry won the Open Class at Stowell on his second outing before being included, at the last minute, in the team for the 1953 European Championships at Badminton. It was his first ever Three-Day Event and he finished in second place. His successes after that are now a legend in eventing lore. He was the mainstay of our successful international teams in the '50s, including the Olympics at Stockholm in 1956 and Rome in 1960.

He was ridden frequently on Salutes and other ceremonial

Troop officers taking part in the Melton
Ride, 1982.

parades, like all the horses who live at The Wood, although by
all accounts he was a 'bit of a lad' and did not take kindly to
slow-moving parades with their accompanying bands and flag-
waving children.

Another Troop officer who has ridden with great success at
high level is Brigadier James Templer. He started his international career on his own horse, M'Lord Connolly, while
serving at The Wood. He has the distinction of winning both
the major Three-Day Events in this country – 1962 at Burghley,
where he won the European Championships, and 1964 at
Badminton. In between he won an international event at
Munich. In 1964 he topped his international career by riding in
the Tokyo Games.

In 1965 Badminton was won by Major E A Boylan on Durlas
Eile. 'Eddie' Boylan served with the Troop from 1946 to 1949,
during which time he competed in the first-ever Badminton.

117

Lieut.-Col W S P (Bill) Lithgow at the Montreal Olympics, 1976. He was Troop Captain from 1956 to 1958 and Commanding Officer from 1958 to 1961 (see photograph opposite, taken at Edinburgh Castle). For many years he was *Chef d'Equipe* of the British Three-Day Event team, and now runs the Pony Club.

Several Troop officers have figured quite prominently as administrators in this most demanding sport. Colonel Weldon acted as *Chef d'Equipe* while still competing and Colonel Bill Lithgow, who commanded The Wood from 1958 to 1961, was *Chef* for no fewer than 12 years during the golden era of British eventing. Without doubt he was one of the all-time 'greats' and certainly played a prominent part in the successful planning of many medal-winning ventures. When Colonel Bill finally retired to become Chairman of the Selection Committee in 1976, he handed over to yet another ex-Troop officer, Tadzic Kopanski. Very soon afterwards Tadzic left the army and I in turn became *Chef*, thus maintaining a long-standing Troop tradition.

To enjoy a tour at The Wood one does not have to win a gold medal or represent Great Britain in an Olympic Games. Just to

(Above) Captain James Templer, *left*, with Her Majesty The Queen at St John's Wood Barracks in 1962.

The Grand Military at Sandown 1984. The author on Burnt Oak leads the field on the first circuit. They eventually came second to HM Queen Elizabeth The Queen Mother's Special Cargo.

The Officers' Mess. The officers (and their dogs) in a jolly mood before a dinner party. Although the Troop is only established for seven officers, from April to the end of the Royal Tournament there are two extra ones, waiting to take over. This photograph shows their welcoming party.

serve in the Troop and to carry out the exciting and fulfilling job we are paid for is an experience of a lifetime. An officer's tour goes only too quickly, and no sooner do you finally reckon that you have got to grips with all the problems of men and horse than you discover that your successor has been nominated, and it is 'days to do'. I feel very fortunate indeed that I have been lucky enough to have served two tours with the Troop, and only wish it could be three. Soon, Reunions and the Royal Tournament will have to replace the daily thrill of being part of it all, and when that happens – as with others who have left these barracks for the last time – the sights and sounds of those flying gun teams will serve to bring back memories of the happiest years of my life.

The Story of 'Jones'

'J' Battery RHA 1914–1919
The Rocket Troop RHA 1914–1928

by COLONEL AK MAIN DSO
who commanded The Rocket Troop
for many years at many stations
at home and abroad, including
St John's Wood.

'Jones' joined J Battery RHA at Aldershot not long before the 1914–18 War. He went to war in the lead of a gun with 'Joubert'. The pair were together throughout the war, and were never 'sick or sorry'.

They were in the lead of the team of the gun that fired the first shell of the war.

After the Armistice they, among many others, were posted to the Rocket Troop in Germany. When I took over the Troop in 1919 they were in the lead of No 4 Gun. In November the Troop came home and all our horses went into quarantine at Swatheling. From there we later marched up to Aldershot.

On arrival at the Square, knowing that we were going into the stables which J Battery had occupied before the war, I told their drivers to let Jones and Joubert (by now renamed Othello) loose, to see where they went. They made straight for their pre-war stable and stalls.

The last time that this grand pair of horses was on parade was at the unveiling of the Gunner War Memorial at Hyde Park Corner, in October 1925. After the parade I obtained sanction from Remounts to pension them off, and Mr Probart, who was then leaving the Rocket Troop, put them out to grass on his land.

During the years 1920–25 they won several prizes in the wheel in Coach Teams and Coaching Marathons, and several Gun Team classes in the lead. They also took part in the RHA Drive at the Royal Tournament for four years.

While at Aldershot Brigadier Willie Clark, then commanding 1st Brigade RHA, chose Jones as his model for a silver statuette of a typical RHA Gun Leader, which he presented to the RA Mess at Aldershot. The statuette is now the property of The King's Troop RHA.

The King's Troop Royal Horse Artillery

COMMANDING OFFICERS

1946	Lt Col H K Gillson, RHA	1965	Maj J M Browell, MBE, RHA
1946	Maj D Welsh, DSO, RHA	1968	Maj A R Rees-Webbe, RHA
1947	Maj J A Norman, DSO, RHA	1971	Maj T J S Eastwood, RHA
1949	Maj F W C Weldon, MVO, MBE, MC, RHA	1973	Maj H B de Fonblanque, RHA
1954	Maj J E Spencer, RHA	1976	Maj R M O Webster, RHA
1956	Maj P H V de C O'Grady, RHA	1978	Maj W R Thatcher, RHA
1958	Maj W S P Lithgow, RHA	1980	Maj R J R Symonds, RHA
1961	Maj P R Heaton-Ellis, RHA	1982	Maj M C R Wallace, RHA

ADJUTANTS

1946	Capt W J W Froud, RHA	1966	Capt R D Kennedy, RHA
1948	Capt W S B Gunn, MC, RHA	1968	Capt J M Beckingsale, MC, RHA
1950	Capt S P H Simonds, MC, RHA	1971	Capt N P S O'Connor, RHA
1953	Capt A I Castle, RHA	1972	Capt G T C Musgrave, RHA
1954	Maj J K I Douglas-Withers, MC, RHA	1975	Capt M Smythe, RHA
1955	Capt J L S Andrews, RHA	1978	Capt N M Cowdery, RHA
1958	Capt J M Farrow, RHA	1981	Capt I A Vere Nicoll, RHA
1960	Capt H D B Hawksley, RHA	1984	Capt N J Foster, RHA
1963	Capt T W Kopanski, RHA		

TROOP CAPTAINS

1946–48	Capt(QM) T M Sutton, RHA	1967–68	Capt T W Kopanski, RHA
1948–50	Capt W S B Gunn, MC, RHA	1968–69	Capt A J Nettleton, RHA
1950–52	Capt B M Ward, MVO, RHA	1969–71	Capt H H Mews, RHA
1952–55	Capt D P H Dyson, RHA	1971–72	Capt W R Thatcher, RHA
1955–56	Maj J K I Douglas-Withers, MC, RHA	1972–73	Capt N P S O'Connor, RHA
1956–58	Maj W S P Lithgow, RHA	1973–76	Capt R J R Symonds, RHA
1958–59	Maj R S MacKenzie, MC, RHA	1976–79	Capt J R L Hodges, RHA
1959–62	Capt P T Holland, MVO, RHA	1979–82	Capt N J Fairley, RHA
1962–67	Capt R W Scott, RHA	1982–	Capt P M Griffith, RHA

SECTION COMMANDERS

	LEFT SECTION		CENTRE SECTION		RIGHT SECTION
1946–49	EA Boylan	1946	B Bazley	1946–47	JA MacDonald
1949–52	PT Holland	1946–48	SPH Simonds	1947–48	PR Body
1952–54	WD Vandeleur	1948–50	JCB Deverill	1948–50	PR Norton
1954–57	JCC Sworder	1950–52	J Cameron-Hayes	1950–51	WD Spiller
1957–61	GDB Thatcher	1952–54	BRW Barber	1951–54	CWD Morgan
1961–64	TJS Eastwood	1954–57	RW Scott	1954–56	SD Pettifer
1964–67	AJ Nettleton	1957–60	JRT Phipps	1956–59	WJ Pinney
1967–70	RMO Webster	1960–63	JR Templer	1959–62	WA Dickens
1970–73	DJM Hall	1963–66	M Hord	1962–65	HB de Fonblanque
1973–76	NA Afford	1966–69	JD Colson	1965–68	RJS Vines
1976–79	MJ Vacher	1969–72	H Palmer	1968–71	WR Thatcher
1979–82	GR Prest	1972–75	JJ Glover	1971–74	MCR Wallace
1982–	MA Houghton	1975–78	LC Tar	1974–77	JD Lang
		1978–81	JR Adderley	1977–80	CL Moore
		1981–84	RM McQ Sykes	1980–83	WE Shaw
		1984–	CJ Seed	1983–	PCH Soar

REGIMENTAL SERGEANT-MAJORS

1946	WOII W Sutton	1965	WOI FWP Hough
1946	WOII R Jackson	1966	WOI GF Stirling, MBE
1950	WOII LG Lungley	1966	WOI W Pearson
1950	WOII CWT Oldham	1972	WOI RN Coshan
1952	WOII J Stewart	1975	WOI JR Emmerson
1956	WOI CWT Oldham	1977	WOI MR Blackmore, BEM
1957	WOI BA Dove	1978	WOI B Friedman
1959	WOII TJ Treen	1981	WOI WG Clarke
1961	WOII GF Stirling, WOI 1962	1984	WOI GP Bailey

CHARTER

1. The King's Troop Royal Horse Artillery is to carry out ceremonial mounted artillery duties as ordered by the General Officer Commanding London District. These duties may be expected to include:

    a. Firing Royal Salutes for Royal Birthdays and Anniversaries, State Openings of Parliament, and State Visits both at Windsor and in London.

    b. Relieving the Household Cavalry Regiment as The Queen's Life Guard during the summer leave period.

    c. Providing a Gun Carriage and team for the funerals of members of the Royal Family and distinguished military officers, and firing Minute Guns during such ceremonies.

    d. Participating in the annual Remembrance Sunday ceremonial.

2. Whenever possible without detriment to the above duties The King's Troop Royal Horse Artillery is to participate in the following events:

    a. The Royal Tournament.

    b. The Lord Mayor's Show.

    c. The Army Benevolent Fund Pageant.

    d. Other parades and shows of a suitable nature.

    e. Equestrian and related competitions.

The level of participation in these events is at the discretion of the officer commanding The King's Troop Royal Horse Artillery, unless over-ruled by the General Officer Commanding London District, and may range from the provision of a lone trumpeter to the performance of the full musical drive.

3. In order to carry out these tasks the officer commanding The King's Troop Royal Horse Artillery is to train and maintain such men and horses as his establishment allows. He is also to maintain:

    a. Seven 13-pounder field guns and limbers.

    b. Harness and stores for gun teams for the above, with an adequate reserve.

4. As far as is compatible with his other duties the officer commanding The King's Troop Royal Horse Artillery is to foster and encourage riding and related pastimes within the Armed Services as a whole and within the Royal Regiment of Artillery in particular.

5. The war role of The King's Troop Royal Horse Artillery is to be as ordered by the General Officer Commanding London District.

6. The King's Troop may also be employed upon tasks in aid of the Civil Community, the Civil Ministries and the Civil Power.

7. The officer commanding The King's Troop Royal Horse Artillery is a commanding officer for disciplinary and administrative purposes. He is under command of the General Officer Commanding London District. In special-to-arm matters he answers to Regimental Headquarters Royal Artillery. His establishment sponsor is Headquarters Director Royal Artillery.

Index

EXPLANATION OF SOME TERMS USED IN THE TEXT

Bottom harness Everyday working harness which has been downgraded from ceremonial or 'top harness', and which is kept in the 'Bottom Harness Room'.

Centre Middle position in a gun team; the 'Ride Centre' on the left is ridden by a 'Centre Driver' while the Hand Centre is on the right.

Detachment The three men who, under command of a Number One, are responsible for bringing a gun into action and firing it. The Number Four is dismounted.

Draught Parade The Troop (or Sections) move out of barracks with the horses in harness pulling the guns, to practise a parade or Drive, train new drivers, etc.

'Hairies' An affectionate term, like 'Fifteen Bobbers', used to describe the 'lines' or team horses.

Hand horse Of the six horses in a team three are ridden and three are led or driven. These hand horses are on the right hand or 'off' side of the team.

Leader The front pair of horses in a gun team are called Leaders.

Limber The two-wheeled 'tender' which is attached to the gun. It was originally designed for ammunition but now carries spare harness.

Lines The name given to the stalls in the Section stables where the team horses are kept.

Remount A young unbroken or partially broken horse.

Rifting A method of cleaning the metal parts of harness to prevent rust.

Shabraque A cloth and gold embellishment to an officer's saddle, over which a sheepskin is placed.

Top harness The harness used on ceremonial occasions which is kept in the 'Top Harness Room'.

Traces Parts of harness made from leather-covered steel wire which join the horses together in a gun team.

Wheeler The rear pair of horses in a team, who not only pull the gun but also act as its brakes.

Author's Note

Very soon after I started writing this book it became apparent that if the Troop was to get the testimony it deserved I was going to need a great deal of help from a lot of people. That help has been readily given by everyone whom I have approached, and I am most grateful to all those kind people who have contributed their time and knowledge and who have generally supported me in this venture.

Firstly I am most grateful to Her Royal Highness The Princess Anne for very generously consenting to write the Foreword.

Colin Cullimore of Dewhurst, The Master Butcher, has been closely associated with the Troop for seven years as a friend and sponsor. During this time Dewhurst's have provided the necessary financial assistance which has allowed the Troop to perform the Musical Drive all over the country. It was natural that I should approach them first when looking for help with this project. The help was immediately forthcoming and I am most grateful to them.

I would like especially to thank Joan Wanklyn, who has been a friend of the Regiment and the Troop for many years. Her contributions to the book – sound advice, painstaking research and wonderful paintings – have been of incalculable value.

I would also like to express my gratitude to General B P Hughes for his precise notes and corrections to my early drafts. I gratefully acknowledge all the help I have received from him and from our other distinguished regimental historians, with particular reference to Brigadier Shelford Bidwell, Lieutenant-Colonel R H C Probert, Brigadier R J Lewendon, Historical Secretary of the Royal Artillery Institution, Mrs Timbers of the Royal Artillery Library, and the dedicated staff of the Royal Artillery Historical Society.

I would like to thank Lieutenant-General Sir Edward Howard-Vyse, Lieutenant-Colonel H M V Nicoll, and Lieutenant-Colonel F W C Weldon for the personal accounts which they have provided of past happenings and people at The Wood.

Kit Houghton, who is one of the country's leading equestrian photographers, has managed to capture the Troop in all its moods under the most trying conditions – I am most grateful to him for his enthusiasm and craftsmanship.

The officers of the King's Troop have been unstinting in their help with the preparation of the book; as have the officers of Headquarters DRA and London District who checked the text and illustrations.

Last, but certainly not least, I would like to thank Barbara Cooper of Threshold Books for her unflagging support and enthusiasm. She and her staff, Suzannah, Kate and Mrs Hastings have not only been extremely tolerant of a 'beginner' but have also made the whole thing fun!

MALCOLM WALLACE,
St John's Wood, 1984

BIBLIOGRAPHY
Bidwell, Brigadier Shelford *The Royal Horse Artillery*
Fonblanque, Major-General E B de *Notes on The Riding Establishment R H A*
Graham, Brigadier C A L *The Story of the Royal Regiment of Artillery*
Hughes, Major-General B P *Honour Titles of The Royal Artillery*
Probert, Lieutenant-Colonel R H C *Some Brief Reference Notes on The Royal Horse Artillery*
Wanklyn, Joan *Guns at the Wood*